Praise for *Leading at a Distance*

"We're living in an unprecedented time that requires a new leadership at every level. Whether you're running a company or a country, there is no playbook for how to engage people and drive meaningful action. But, through work like Leading at a Distance, *we can learn from each other and find new ways of working, living, and leading."*

Hans Vestberg,
Chairman and CEO Verizon

"Remote work is here to stay; now comes the hard work of making it sustainable and inclusive. Leading at a Distance *offers a roadmap. Jim and Darleen – both experts in their own right – cull timely research and insights from a who's-who of business leaders into a compact and actionable guide that you'll turn to again and again."*

Rachel Thomas,
CEO, LeanIn.Org

"Leading at a Distance *is remarkably timely, a much-needed tool for any business leader in a post-COVID world. You'd be foolish not to read this book. Citrin and DeRosa not only help adapt your organization to successful distance work. They also offer first aid to the crumbling corporate culture in the aftermath of this global pandemic."*

Martin Lindstrom,
New York Times best-selling author,
Buyology and *The Ministry of Common Sense*

"*The COVID-19 pandemic changed the way we work . . . maybe permanently.* Leading at a Distance *provides helpful insight on how to stay connected, build trust, coach teams, and drive talent innovation in a virtual world.*"

Carol Tome,
CEO, UPS

"*In* Leading at a Distance *Jim Citrin and Darleen DeRosa offer practical and cutting-edge leadership thinking for the new digital world accelerated by the global pandemic. This book is a must-read for sitting CEOs and leadership teams who will find the relevant tools to manage in an increasingly virtual environment.*"

Dambisa Moyo,
Global Economist; author,
How Boards Work and *How the West Was Lost*

"*It's always a challenge for leaders to stay nimble as technology upends the old way of doing business, and the era we're living in is no different. But they'll find lots of great advice in Citrin and DeRosa's timely new book – a primer for how to lead in a flexible and dynamic work environment.*"

David Solomon,
CEO, Goldman Sachs

"*As virtual work is here to stay,* Leading at a Distance *should be required reading for us all. Illuminating the pitfalls of virtual work, Citrin and DeRosa nonetheless show us a path to navigating work at a distance with both enjoyment and success.*"

Betsy Bradley,
President, Vassar College

"*Virtual, or remote, leadership is a timely topic. Fortunately for us, authors Citrin and DeRosa began their research 15 years earlier, and their wisdom will remain with us for decades to come.*"

Satya Nadella,
CEO, Microsoft

"*From employee onboarding and ongoing engagement, to reimagining company processes and reinforcing culture,* Leading at a Distance *offers timely insights and tools for leaders at all levels to help redefine what it means to connect and lead in a virtual or hybrid workplace. A must-read leadership guide for navigating this new paradigm to cultivate stronger teams and deliver greater results in these new workplace environments.*"

Gail Boudreaux,
President and CEO, Anthem

"Leading at a Distance *could not be more timely to help organizations, leaders, and employees thrive in today's remote work environment. Perhaps more importantly, this book, with its deep research basis and compelling insights brought to life with vivid examples, will become a timeless resource as all of our relationships with work will continue to meaningfully change.*"

John Donahoe,
CEO, Nike

"*Many leaders have adjusted well to a virtual world but on the basis of tweaking approaches that worked in a physical one.* Leading at a Distance *flips that paradigm, starting with remote as the standard and designing everything from communication strategy to onboarding to running effective meetings with a virtual-first mindset. Citrin and DeRosa's insights are both critical now and sure to have lasting value in a post-pandemic world.*"

Rich Lesser,
CEO, BCG

"*Human capital is the lifeline of every organization, and among the most valued assets in corporate America. Now more than ever, keeping talent motivated and engaged is a critical key to success. In* Leading at a Distance, *James Citrin and Darleen DeRosa give leaders the tools to effectively inspire their teams during the pandemic and* beyond. *This book brings excellent best practices for corporations looking to thrive in a virtual world.*"

Mellody Hobson,
Co-CEO and President, Ariel Investments

"*Jim Citrin and Darleen DeRosa know more great leaders than any combination of authors I have ever met and* Leading at a Distance *combines the wisdom they have accumulated over the years with their incredible learning in the past year.* Leading at a Distance *will be a guidebook for leaders long after today's crisis. I am going to recommend it to every leader I know!*"

Marshall Goldsmith, top-rated executive coach
in the world for over a decade and #1
New York Times best-selling author,
Triggers and *What Got You Here Won't Get You There*

"Leading at a Distance *is an essential guide to the many ways in which the year of COVID will transform the way we work.*"

Mark Thompson,
Former CEO, *New York Times*; author,
Enough Said: What's Gone Wrong with the Language of Politics

"*In* Leading at a Distance, *Jim Citrin and Darleen DeRosa share their key learnings for how the most successful organizations balance the benefits of both in-person and virtual work environments to keep employees engaged and productive. Their insights and leadership lessons from top business leaders could not be more timely.*"

Adam Silver,
Commissioner, NBA

"*Citrin's passion for leadership and DeRosa's knowledge of virtual teams results in a powerful combination of practical tips for operating in a future that will no doubt feature more remote work. Rather than debate how much more remote work there will be, we should all adopt the principles outlined in this how-to guide for* Leading at a Distance."

Carlos Rodriguez,
CEO, ADP

"Leading at a Distance *provides unmatched access to the real, lived experiences of business leaders as they deal with profound changes to professional life. In expert fashion, Citrin and DeRosa crystallize new responsibilities and possibilities for virtual leadership.*"

Toni Petersson,
CEO, Oatly

"*A brilliantly timed book! Jim Citrin and Darleen DeRosa have produced an unmatched playbook for leading in the virtual workplace.* Leading at a Distance *offers tactical advice that is easy to digest and fun to read. It is written with the confidence of two leading experts in the field and filled with examples that make the content both credible and relatable. As businesses move from virtual to a hybrid model in the post-COVID-19 world, Citrin and DeRosa offer the go-to guide for how to be successful. This book should be required reading for every CEO and executive.*"

Jared Cohen,
CEO, Jigsaw, Google; *New York Times*
best-selling author, *The New Digital Age:
Transforming Nations, Businesses, and Our Lives*

"Leading at a Distance *is the essential, very practical, immediately useful manual all of us need to get better at leading in this new, permanently changed environment. The world will be a better place thanks to Citrin and DeRosa's new book.*"

Hubert Joly, Former Chairman and CEO,
Best Buy; author, *The Heart of Business:
Leadership Principles for the Next Era of Capitalism*

"*Without a doubt, technology has enabled leaders to meaningfully connect and manage throughout the pandemic. As working from anywhere is here to stay,* Leading at a Distance *is a timely guide to tackle how to navigate this new normal while fostering team growth, connectivity, and inclusivity – all in service of driving strong results. Success in virtual leadership requires leaders to treat the environment as an* opportunity and this book provides insights, applications and tools to do just that."

Mary Dillon,
CEO, Ulta Beauty

"Leading at a Distance *is an essential read for every leader navigating today's rapidly changing work environment. Jim and Darleen draw on their deep expertise to provide invaluable insights on the elements of successful virtual leadership. Their book is a timely and necessary toolkit for leaders working to build trust, collaboration, and productivity as we enter the future of work.*"

Dan Schulman,
CEO, PayPal

"Leading at a Distance *could not have come at a better time. Becoming adept at virtual meetings has become the only way to survive throughout 2020. Citrin and DeRosa offer ways to ensure that leaders not only survive but thrive in the world of virtual work. The book offers ways to excel at leading in a virtual work environment and provides rich examples of how to motivate and inspire a remote workforce.*"

Gail McGovern,
President and CEO,
American Red Cross

"*Leading effectively, already tough in today's uncertain and ambiguous context, faces compounding challenges in the virtual setting. Drawing from fresh practices innovated by corporations and startups to decades of research on managing and teaming,* Leading at a Distance *gives us an actionable blueprint for success in virtual leadership. One of the toughest aspects to leading is closing the perception, knowledge, and emotional distance between leaders and those whom they lead through communications and feedback. This book amps up our superpowers in doing that, even when we are leading at a distance.*"

Sanyin Siang,
Thinkers50 #1 Coach and
Mentor; Professor, Duke University

"The future of work will require more from leaders. Success will be driven by those who build trust, equity, and a work experience that matches the values of their company and their employees. Leading at a Distance *is a powerful tool for success in this new world."*

Jamie Iannone,
CEO, eBay

"Virtual working, in multiple different forms, is here to stay. Leading at a Distance *is not just an excellent playbook for how to get the most out of this new sport. It also addresses the key question of how to simultaneously build the social capital that organisations and teams need to win in the COVID post season."*

Alan Jope,
CEO, Unilever

LEADING

AT A DISTANCE

JAMES M. CITRIN

DARLEEN DEROSA

LEADING

PRACTICAL LESSONS

FOR VIRTUAL SUCCESS

AT A DISTANCE

WILEY

Published by John Wiley & Sons, Inc., Hoboken, New Jersey.

Published simultaneously in Canada.

For general information on our other products and services or for technical support, please contact our Customer Care Department within the United States at (800) 762-2974, outside the United States at (317) 572-3993 or fax (317) 572-4002.

Wiley publishes in a variety of print and electronic formats and by print-on-demand. Some material included with standard print versions of this book may not be included in e-books or in print-on-demand. If this book refers to media such as a CD or DVD that is not included in the version you purchased, you may download this material at http://booksupport.wiley.com. For more information about Wiley products, visit www.wiley.com.

Library of Congress Cataloging-in-Publication Data is Available:

ISBN 9781119782445 (Hardcover)
ISBN 9781119782469 (ePDF)
ISBN 9781119782452 (ePub)

Cover Design: Wiley

SKY10026006_040221

To my beloved Lindsay
—J.C.

To Joe, Drew, and Natalie, with love
—D.D.

Contents

Preface: "The Most Obscure PhD in History": The Story Behind This Book

"That has to be the single most obscure PhD in history."

Those were my first words to Darleen DeRosa, when I was introduced to her in January of 2020. We were in the Stamford, Connecticut, office of Spencer Stuart, one of the world's leading global leadership advisory and executive search firms. For 27 years I've had the pleasure of working at Spencer Stuart, the worldwide leader in CEO, board, and C-suite executive recruiting and leadership, organizational, and culture advisory services, channeling my passion of connecting with and building the very best talent. Darleen had just been recruited as a core member of our Leadership Advisory Services Practice. For the prior dozen years, Darleen led a highly specialized advisory firm, OnPoint Consulting, after having served as an executive director in the assessment practice of another leading firm.

Darleen explained that she had long been passionate about the topic of virtual teams as a part of her broader interest in leadership development and succession planning. In fact, when she was doing her doctoral work in social/organizational psychology at Temple University, her subspecialty was how to build, manage, optimize, and create cultures for virtual teams.

"I think that virtual leadership will become increasingly important as remote work becomes even more prevalent in the

future," Darleen said. "Right now, about 10% of employees in the U.S. work remotely, and projections suggest that by 2025 that number could *double* to 20%!"

Okay, that is all fine and well, I thought at the time. But the issue didn't feel that relevant to me personally.

How the world changed! Only a couple of months later, as COVID-19 became a global pandemic, Darleen's expertise rocketed from the periphery to the epicenter of our world. In late February 2020, in a staff meeting, Darleen gave a training session on virtual leadership, including some critical basics, such as how to facilitate and lead a virtual meeting. Immediately, Darleen became a rock star and in heavy demand by our clients around the world. Within weeks, she was a keen differentiator as we were advising boards and senior executives in real time as they were navigating some of the most critical leadership moments of their careers.

Directly applying lessons from Darleen, we were able to shift much of our work at Spencer Stuart and seamlessly advise clients on virtual leadership – by then a ubiquitous challenge. Thanks to that, we were able to keep our business operating, and move our CEO, board director, C-suite executive searches, and succession planning assignments forward effectively during the early and uncertain pandemic days of March and April 2020.

That summer, knowing that I have long been a student of leadership, CEO succession, and executive success, Darleen called and asked if I would co-author a book on virtual leadership. She shared that a senior editor at John Wiley & Sons had called suggesting that she update her 2010 book, *Virtual Success: A Practical Guide for Working and Leading from a Distance*.

I was thrilled. From that time on, we dove in together to create *Leading at a Distance*. The process of researching and writing the book has been a fun and incredibly helpful learning journey. I've applied the lessons on staying connected, building trust, coaching, and innovating with our Spencer Stuart CEO Practice team, composed of Melissa Stone, Hannah Ford, Ashley Zaslav, Karen Steinegger, and Maddi Conlin. That has been the very best part of working remotely. I feel we are all more in synch and effective than ever, although I really miss our team dinners. And similarly, I was able to lead a wide variety of CEO searches and succession projects, from eBay to Virgin Galactic, completely virtually, by following all the practices outlined in this book.

Both Darleen and I hope that you enjoy this book – and more importantly, that you apply it to accelerate your own professional success and the achievements and satisfaction of your teams and organizations.

Jim Citrin, November 2020

During college at Holy Cross, I always thought that I would become a clinical psychologist. After college, I worked in a clinical setting at Yale University School of Medicine for several years and realized that I could apply the same practices in consulting, where I could blend two topics that I enjoyed – people and business. This led me to pursue a PhD in organizational psychology.

At that time, in the early 2000s, companies like AT&T and others began using virtual collaboration. I told my doctoral advisor that I wondered whether teams that worked virtually could be as effective as co-located teams. This wasn't just a theoretical question: I wanted to study *real* teams inside *real* companies. While I was conducting research for my PhD, I asked consulting firms to let me survey their clients. Eventually Steve Krupp at Right Management Consultants brought me on as an intern to conduct a global study. This internship quickly turned into a full-time consulting job, and that research became one of the first applied studies on this topic.

My fascination with virtual work continued. At OnPoint Consulting, the executive succession and leadership development firm I launched in 2008, we conducted three more global studies on virtual teams, which were by then becoming increasingly common. We strove to identify what differentiated the best virtual leaders and teams from the rest. Over the next 12-plus years, we consulted with numerous clients and helped them better equip their virtual leaders for success. After publishing my first book on this topic, *Virtual Success: A Practical Guide for Working and Leading from a Distance* (with Rick Lepsinger), we applied our experience to craft an array of leadership development programs for virtual leaders – which we eventually delivered in a "virtual" classroom.

When I joined Spencer Stuart in January 2020 to continue my emphasis on CEO succession, I thought my passion for virtual leadership would be put on hold. Little did I know that just two months later, we would face a global crisis where organizations had to pivot quickly to a virtual setting. On our firm's website, we published an article, "Leading from a Distance: 5 Lessons for Virtual Teaming," and clients began asking for us to help them learn to operate in this new environment. Jim began sharing my articles on LinkedIn and inviting me to meetings with his clients to talk about their challenges working in this new normal.

When Wiley called to ask me to write a new book, my first inclination was to say no, given how busy I was with client work and the kids at home. However, I realized that this was the exact moment when leaders and companies needed these insights more than ever. What Jim referred to as "the most obscure PhD" was highly relevant to a broader audience. I also realized that Jim's passion for leadership, coupled with his interest in the topic (and the fact that he has written seven books), made him a great co-author. Whenever we had a question, Jim called CEOs or other top leaders to get an insider's perspective. A fun example of this is when we were reading about new advancements in Microsoft Teams to combat video fatigue, Jim contacted Satya Nadella and Kathleen Hogan, CEO and CHRO of Microsoft, respectively, who put us in direct touch with Jeff Teper, the leader of the product, design, and engineering teams for Microsoft 365, which includes Microsoft Teams.

Working on the book virtually with our superb internal project team (Ashley Zaslav, Hannah Ford, and Will Dowling) has also been an opportunity for us to test out new approaches. We navigated learning how to leverage different technologies and channel flexibility. Some of us took video calls from our kids' playroom or a hospital room with a relative; one of us sent notes while out at sea on a boat in Bermuda, all the while learning more about each other as people and employees.

What I love most about this book is that it integrates more than 15 years of research and experience in a practical way that anyone can apply. We hope that you enjoy this labor of love.

Darleen DeRosa, November 2020

Introduction: The Virtual Revolution

A t the start, we were all operating on adrenaline.

When the COVID-19 global pandemic broke in early 2020, millions of organizations and hundreds of millions of employees shifted on a dime to working remotely. A can-do spirit set in individually and collectively, fueled by the once-in-a-generation sense of shared humanity, driving people around the world to adapt and perform at unimaginably high levels of productivity. Employee engagement scores increased as CEOs and corporate leaders stepped up and communicated with much greater frequency, transparency, and authenticity than they had felt appropriate before the crisis set in. And a great many office workers, powered by Zoom, Teams, WebEx, and BlueJeans, quickly found joys in working from home and eliminating the grind of the daily commute and business travel.

A year later, much of this novelty had washed away.

This is not only about Zoom burnout. Fear and uncertainty about the virus and the resulting global economic collapse, concerns about the well-being of loved ones, and job insecurity were further exacerbated by the many other afflictions of *Annus Horribilis* 2020. The all-too-well-known list includes historic levels of political polarization, nationwide protests over racial injustice ignited by the killing of George Floyd, and record-destructive wildfires throughout the West Coast of the United States, just to

name a few. And the work-from-home (WFH) trend, which was a part of many professionals' working lives pre-COVID-19 but dramatically accelerated when companies closed offices due to the pandemic, will remain both a privilege and source of ongoing stress, taxing mental health, putting pressure on personal relationships, and uncovering new challenges for employees and their leaders alike.

Someday the COVID-19 pandemic will end – and we hope you are reading this book from that vantage point. But even as we write this, at a time when "social distancing" remains an imperative and few companies are encouraging or even letting workers return to offices (with masks on), this much is clear: we are in the early days of a dramatic, long-term shift in how work is done. In this emerging world, the work of leaders will less frequently occur face-to-face, and more of it will be done virtually, whether by means of audio, video, email, text, Slack, Teams, or whatever new technologies emerge. Our goal with *Leading at a Distance* is to share highly practical insights for how to be the best virtual leader you can be. Given that an important aspect of leadership is role modeling, it will also be important to share advice about how to be the most effective virtual employee you can be.

Our insights are based on deep academic and professional research on the topic of virtual leadership, coupled with our fieldwork from partnering with many of the most successful CEOs, business leaders, and organizations around the world. We have interviewed (virtually, of course) over 100 CEOs, CHROs, and top business leaders for this book, surveyed thousands of individuals and companies, and applied our own observations as practitioners advising boards and companies on leadership selection, executive assessment and development, CEO succession, and board governance.

Luckily, there are effective ways both to work and to lead at a distance. And in the coming years, we believe that leaders' ability to master these skills of leadership will mean the difference between individual and organizational success and failure.

Accelerating an Existing Trend: Virtual Work Is Here to Stay

To set the stage, let us share some foundational data. Prior to COVID-19, our survey of HR and talent leaders from over 150 companies showed that virtual work was not a rare phenomenon – 13% of the workforce, on average, was considered fully remote. When we resurveyed CHROs and rewards and talent leaders over a span of two weeks in July and August 2020 in which leaders from 55 organizations participated, that percentage skyrocketed to over 60% at the end of March 2020 and reached well in excess of 80% as of August 2020.

Looking ahead, these same HR and talent leaders anticipate that nearly half of their employees will continue to work from home even when things have stabilized. Another study by Northeastern University's *Experience* magazine[1] found that 80% of employees who were new to remote work reported that they wanted to continue to work remotely at least part time in the future (although only 15% said they would want to do so full time), and those who had already been working remotely before COVID-19 were even more enthusiastic about continuing to work remotely.

A 2020 McKinsey and Leanin.org Women in the Workplace report[2] showed that the COVID-19 crisis led many organizations to rethink remote work. The report indicated that 93% of companies say that more jobs can be done remotely, and 67% predict many employees will regularly work remotely in the future. Further, almost 8 in 10 employees reported that they want to continue to work remotely more often than before.

The point is that virtual work is no longer a temporary phenomenon in our lives, but rather a long-term transformation in how millions of people will work and how most organizations will function. Virtual work is here to stay.

A Tale of Three Perspectives

One of the most extraordinary things about the rapid shift to remote work in early 2020 was how universal it was. No matter who you talked to, nearly every professional who normally works in an office was going through the shift to remote work together. Those who were not making the shift were risking their lives as first responders or continuing their duties as

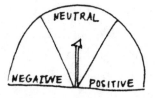

essential workers – and for all these heroes, we are deeply thankful. Their corporate counterparts were only able to do their work from home because they kept our society functioning and moving forward.

Navigating the shift meant managers had to learn how to keep their teams running through videoconferences, colleagues had to figure out how to design or develop products while not being physically together, or professionals had to learn how to advise, sell, and service clients remotely. We were all going through it on a personal basis too. Most people were forced to abandon their plans and rituals and find new routines. Families turned to celebrating holidays, birthdays, and even weddings over Zoom, and there was an explosion of self-recorded video tributes. People talked about living in lockdown and how it was all working for them the way that they've talked about the weather for millennia.

But that is not to suggest that everyone was experiencing life and work the same way. Far from it. As one example, in research from LeanIn.org,[3] working mothers have been doing significantly more caregiving and housework than men during the pandemic, and as a result, they've been showing signs of burnout and anxiety. Among women and men who have full-time jobs, partners, and children, women have been spending an average of *20 hours* more per week than men on childcare, housework, and caring for relatives. This is the equivalent of an extra part-time job. Another group hit hard has been young, single urbanites, who were forced to work from small apartments. This cohort reported far greater levels of isolation and depression, not surprisingly, than executives and wealthy senior professionals working from second homes with well-equipped home offices.

In general, leaders at all levels felt the shift, too. Based on our surveys, only about a quarter of CEOs believe that the shift to remote work has been a net positive for them individually compared to a surprisingly high 61% of non-CEOs, who said that remote work has been positive. However, the great majority of both CEOs and non-CEOs report much higher levels of personal stress as a result of the shift to remote work in their organizations. Furthermore, leaders acknowledge that their personal connections with colleagues have been negatively impacted by remote work.

Both CEOs and other leaders report that they are more productive as a result of working remotely. Over three-quarters of CEOs and 90 percent of other leaders report being more productive or equally productive as compared to their usual in-office routine, and both populations agree that technology experience and access to learning and development opportunities have been positively impacted by remote work.

This, in turn, has enabled advances in leaders' ability to communicate with and inspire employees, which has fostered improved innovation, collaboration, and teamwork. And while no one expects CEOs to have great work-life balance (or sympathizes with them if they don't), CEOs report that the shift to remote work has been about neutral on their work-life balance, due to the elimination of customer and client travel and fewer (if any) in-person management, board, and investor meetings. On the other hand, among the broader group of leaders we surveyed, 60% of leaders report that their work-life balance has shifted in a positive direction.

The key goal is to build on the benefits of virtual leadership and overcome its disadvantages.

As we watched how companies adapted to the sudden, pandemic-driven need to work from home, and how leaders were assessing the potential for this trend to remain or increase after the pandemic eases, we identified three distinct perspectives:

The First Perspective: Net Positive

An inspiring example of the net positive is Kenya-based Jessica Posner Odede, CEO of the global not-for-profit, Girl Effect (on which Jim is a board director), who shared with us that she has experienced game-changing benefits from the shift to remote work. We spoke to Jess to learn how she's used leading at a distance to reimagine how the entire organization operates. Girl Effect's mission is to empower girls around the world through youth brands and mobile platforms to change their lives. Focused on designing girl-centered technology, they create content and products that millions of girls, particularly those in Africa and India, use in ways that encourage their health and well-being. Rather than managing the organization and making decisions from a centralized headquarter office in London, where the organization had been based before Jess became CEO in 2019, Jess created a distributed organization, with colleagues on three continents. Prior to COVID-19, Jess moved to Nairobi herself (with her Kenyan husband, Kennedy Odede). The most critical lesson for Jess coming out of 2020 is that it's not just about how you lead a virtual team, but it's about taking the organization to your consumers and rethinking the delivery to dramatically increase your impact.

Other companies are following this principle of changing how the business operates to adapt to the times. Sandeep Mathrani, CEO of flex space behemoth WeWork, for example, told us how he is adapting the business to the times. Before COVID-19, WeWork's main focus was its turnaround – streamlining the organization's overhead expenses and optimizing its real estate portfolio. But as the pandemic took control of the industry, WeWork's strategy shifted to diversifying its member base beyond the company's traditional start-up and enterprise customers. As a result the company moved to digitize its core workspace product through subscription and on-demand models while also targeting industries like higher education and life sciences, which, regardless of the pandemic, are in need of innovative space solutions.

Tim Cook, CEO of Apple, which invested an estimated $5 billion to create its space-age Apple Park campus in 2017, has been quoted[4] in the press that he was both surprised and impressed by employees' ability to operate remotely. In 2020, the company created products, including new Apple Watches and iPads, that launched on time, even though most employees were working away from the office. He said that Apple will not return to the way they were, "because we've found that there are some things that actually work really well virtually."

The Second Perspective: Net Negative

Of course, not every business leader is so sanguine about remote work. Netflix's Reed Hastings has called remote work "a pure negative."[5] Jamie Dimon, CEO of JPMorgan Chase, who started working again from the bank's New York headquarters in June 2020, said he sees social as well as economic damage from longer stretches of working from home. During public appearances, Jamie indicated that he believes that remote work is no substitute for in-person interaction, and he has seen alienation among younger workers. As a result, the bank started bringing workers back to the office in significant numbers in the fall of 2020. Many other CEOs we interviewed for the book would agree, especially at companies that either design and manufacture physical products, like Nike, or that have notable apprenticeship cultures, such as Goldman Sachs.

In addition, many people find working remotely extremely taxing. There are more meetings, more time on Zoom, and greater demands for managers to check in with their teams. Workloads have also expanded, with more emails (+5%), more emails sent outside business hours (+8%), and many more meetings (+13%), all combining to extend the workday by an average of 48 minutes.[6] Jill Hooley, professor of psychology at Harvard and lead author of the classic textbook *Abnormal Psychology*, has studied managing depression in the workplace and the impact of remote work. "You hardly need me to tell you that we are dealing with very challenging times," she told us. "Even the most successful business leaders may have family members or colleagues who have lost their jobs or who are dealing with other threats to their economic security." She added that there are also the stresses that come from loss: "the loss of loved ones for some people, loss of our regular routines and favorite activities for everyone, as well as the stress that comes from loss of normalcy."

The Third Perspective: Somewhere in the Middle

Yet for many others, the move to remote work has been somewhere in the middle. Kathleen Hogan, of Microsoft, shared that "working remotely has ushered in the best of times and the worst of times." There have been some real positives, such as productivity. At a personal level, Kathleen has not had to commute to the company's Redmond, Washington, headquarters and has had much more time to work – and to be around her college-aged son, who has been attending classes remotely. She added that for many of the company's leaders, such as those who work with enterprise customers and governments around the world, the velocity of business has accelerated dramatically, enabled by the fact that the norm of traveling to visit customers has been replaced by video meetings. One of the top officers of Microsoft said, "I've met with five governments today," doing in days what typically took weeks. Similarly, Kathleen conducts best-practices sessions with peer CHROs, which she used to do in person. Those meetings would normally have taken so much time to schedule and now it's much faster to get them set and executed. "Last week I spoke with a half a dozen CHROs about what they're experiencing," she said. At an organizational level, remote work at Microsoft has led to a level of flexibility she and other company leaders never thought was possible. "It's allowed us to tap into diverse talent, access and hire more people from different geographies, and be incredibly productive along the way," she said.

At the same time, Kathleen shares the sentiment expressed by almost all the other leaders we spoke with: There is no substitute for being in person. "A big aspect of being with other people is the serendipity that often presents itself in life." She worries about that loss both individually and organizationally. Employees seem to agree that there is something to be said for the hybrid approach. "While we continue to learn, our current research shows roughly 80% of our employees want to go back to the office, but with greater flexibility, while roughly 20% say they want to work from home all the time. Some thought the 80/20 rule would be in favor of people wanting to work from home given COVID and we are seeing the opposite."

We interviewed Jamie Iannone, CEO of eBay, who agrees. There have been some massive advantages to remote work, but some serious disadvantages as well. One surprising benefit for Jamie was the way it accelerated his onboarding process when he joined the company in April 2020, after having been the successful candidate in a CEO search that was conducted predominantly virtually. "It's remarkable how efficient and effective we can be," he said. "When I started, I wanted to visit all of our offices around the world. In normal times that would have been a multi-week process. Now it was achieved in a matter of days. And it was easy to customize my communications to the audience. I just changed my virtual background to that of our German office, UK office, Amsterdam office, and everywhere else I visited."

Yet despite articulating many of the benefits, Jamie concluded that working remotely has been a slight net negative. He knows that connecting with people is a huge part of leadership and he misses managing by walking around, having the three-minute conversations in the halls, elevators, or cafeteria. For him, working remotely while coming into the company from outside – Jamie had been COO of Walmart's gigantic e-commerce business – has created challenges building new relationships. "It's relatively easy and efficient to translate a 3D relationship into 2D, but it's hard just to start and build a meaningful relationship in 2D."

Our Perspective: Working and Leading at a Distance Is Here to Stay

Let us share our point of view directly at this point. We believe that a minority of companies will attempt to go all the way back to how things were and revert to the formal in-the-office-everyday model they had pre-COVID-19. Similarly, we also believe that only a minority will shift toward full work-from-home or the even more permissive work-from-anywhere (WFA) model that lets people relocate and telecommute from less expensive or more idyllic environments. Yes, a few large tech companies have announced this shift. However, we believe most companies and organizations will wind up with some version of a hybrid model.

On average, professionals will still have an office, visit clients, and conduct some business face to face, but they're almost certain to spend fewer hours in this mode than they did prior to 2020. As a result, *everyone* will be required to try to improve their remote leadership and working skills. Whether you're based in a high-rise or an office park 10 days a year or 100 days a year, you will need to get better at doing all the things your role requires on those days that you or your teams are working from the home office. The number of hours a year you are likely to spend leading virtually is probably going to spike in a permanent and meaningful way.

Learning to lead virtually isn't the only priority. To succeed, leaders must understand how to thrive as individuals working at a distance. This will require creating new systems and routines for you as an individual to address the things that are gone because of the lack of the structure of the office. You'll need to figure out how to be productive and deliver results while staying healthy, engaged, and sane.

The Big Questions

Moving forward, leaders and organizations are all confronting a series of important issues:

- How to optimize the impact of virtual leadership
- How to help employees have the most positive experiences so that their organizations can deliver the most positive results on a sustainable basis
- How to hire, train, coach, and promote employees virtually on an ongoing basis that lets them integrate into the fabric of the organization and thrive
- How to shift business models and organizational structures as the world continues to evolve

- How to think about the return to the office and the future of work in a post-COVID-19 world
- How to evolve corporate cultures from a distance
- And how, on an individual basis, to retain the energy, vitality, and enthusiasm that are needed in organizations and the world more than ever

Until now, there has not been a research-based, practical resource available to address these questions and guide leaders who must engage and lead from a distance. The objective of this book is to fill that gap and provide a hands-on, effective toolkit for organizations and leaders of remote employees and virtual teams. While this book can certainly be read from cover to cover, we recommend that you also use it as a chapter-by-chapter reference, making it your go-to guide for virtual leadership.

We believe that the common perception that remote work will never be as effective as work in traditional, face-to-face teams is false. Many companies we have worked with have already developed highly successful strategies for working in virtual teams. And some of the innovations and advantages are not possible in a physically proximate environment. Thanks to those companies, as well as our extensive research and consulting in this area, we have learned many helpful insights and best practices. By sharing our findings in this book, we hope to empower you to help your organization create a successful and dynamic virtual environment.

Notes

1 Schuyler Velasco, "Offices will reopen soon. Here's what workers really want," *Experience*, May 27, 2020, https://expmag.com/2020/05/offices-will-reopen-soon-heres-what-workers-really-want/.

2 "Women are maxing out and burning out during COVID-19," Leanin.org, May 7, 2020, https://leanin.org/article/womens-workload-and-burnout.

3 Ibid.

4 Mark Gurman, "Apple CEO Tim Cook happy with remote work, says some things 'work really well virtually,'" *The Print*, September 22, 2020, https://theprint.in/tech/apple-ceo-tim-cook-happy-with-remote-work-says-some-things-work-really-well-virtually/507829/.

5 Joe Flint, "Netflix's Reed Hastings Deems Remote Work 'a Pure Negative,'" *Wall Street Journal*, September 7, 2020, www.wsj.com/articles/netflixs-reed-hastings-deems-remote-work-a-pure-negative-11599487219.

6 Jeff Green, "The average pandemic workday is 48 minutes longer and has more meetings, shows research," *Economic Times*, August 4, 2020, https://economictimes.indiatimes.com/jobs/the-average-pandemic-workday-is-48-minutes-longer-and-has-more-meetings-shows-research/articleshow/77342816.cms?from=mdr.

1

What We Learned from the Pandemic: Our Research Shows Remote Work Is Here to Stay

During normal times, Starbucks opens a new store in China every 15 hours. But in late January 2020, as executives at its regional headquarters in Shanghai began hearing reports of a highly contagious new virus spreading in Wuhan and beyond, the team had to make an uncharacteristic decision: to *close* all its 4,300 stores in China to prevent the spread of the illness, and to send all 58,000 employees home.

Like other multinationals with a strong presence in China, Starbucks' operations there gave it an early warning of how seriously COVID-19 might affect its locations and communities around the globe. But when COVID-19 began forcing U.S. companies to close their doors and shift to remote work in mid-March, Starbucks was still, in some ways, ill prepared. "Because we're a relationship-driven company, we've never done a great job supporting people who've wanted to work remotely," said Lucy Helms in an interview. (Before retiring at the end of 2020, Lucy was Starbucks' chief human resources officer.) For instance, the company had more than 50 software systems that supported remote work, but partly because there were so many options, few employees knew how to use them effectively. Quickly, Starbucks' tech group, led by Chief Technology Officer Gerri Martin-Flickinger, created crash courses in Microsoft Teams. Before long, everyone became comfortable using it for video meetings, file sharing, and group chat. Soon Starbucks' employees' instinct to get work done kicked in. They'd seen how Starbucks' stores in China had reopened within two months, so they treated those early weeks of working from spare bedrooms and kitchen tables as a sprint. "When we first went remote, we all assumed it was a short-term thing," Lucy said. That optimism turned out to be premature.

Still, as Lucy looked back months later and assessed Starbucks' rapid shift to all-remote work, she saw many positive signs. Engagement scores, as measured by pulse surveys, remained high. So did productivity. Employees gave leaders high marks for accessibility and authenticity. The HR team moved quickly to answer all sorts of unanticipated questions from employees, coming up with new policies to answer queries such as "Can I use sick time for homeschooling?"

As the pandemic dragged on, one question came up repeatedly from the 4,500 employees who work at Starbucks' headquarters in Seattle. REI, a large retailer with a newly opened headquarters in nearby Bellevue, announced plans to sell its building and let its employees work remotely even after the pandemic. Some Starbucks employees wanted to know: Can we do that too?

To Lucy, the answer was clear. "We've stated, 'No, we'll never be all remote,'" she said. Starbucks is a brand built on in-person experiences, and its corporate culture values apprenticeship and mentorship that's harder to do at a distance. Lucy says Starbucks imagines a hybrid future, with some employees in the office and others remote most days. She recognizes that will create new challenges. "Leading hybrid teams is harder," she said. In fact, her HR team's next important task is equipping managers to meet that challenge.

"If there is an office in the future," wrote Charles Handy in a 1995 *Harvard Business Review* article[1] on virtual work, "it will be more like a clubhouse: a place for meeting, eating, and greeting, with rooms reserved for activities, not for particular people." Admittedly, most organizations have not reached that point yet, but the way we work has certainly changed dramatically since Handy's predictions. Before the pandemic, some organizations instituted telecommuting and created "hoteling" options for employees who visit the office only occasionally. Now, as hybrid forms of work grow more common, most organizations are preparing to adapt to virtual work as the new normal.

History will look back on the pandemic as a dramatic accelerator of this trend. Most CEOs and CHROs we interviewed for *Leading at a Distance* take pride in the fact that they were able to move thousands of employees to working from home in a matter of days. The dramatic shift was made possible by the technology infrastructure that had been built up over recent years. No technology company saw its usage jump more dramatically than Zoom, whose market capitalization rose tenfold to $160 billion between January and October 2020.[2]

But even before COVID-19, there were reasons why some organizations were expanding their reliance on virtual work. In the war for talent, many organizations have realized that they need to hunt further afield for the very best talent and create the conditions that allow them to work from afar without relocating. Being able to hire people who live anywhere is also a major advantage for organizations pursuing increased diversity in their workforces. McKinsey and Leanin.org's Women in the Workplace study[3] found that 70% of the companies reported that remote work will allow them to increase the diversity in their hiring practices. In addition, the report illustrated that remote work expands options for employees who are caregivers or who have disabilities that interfere with travel or long commutes.

The second reason for the increase in virtual work is the combination of technology advances and globalization. Multinationals have always had to develop systems to manage through distributed organizational structures and share information to keep things on track. However, as technology has increased people's ability to work together virtually, instead of having a separate team run each of a company's operations in different countries or regions, firms have increasingly used distributed teams to work together across locations and time zones to capitalize on shifts in the marketplace, innovate, and bring new products to market.

Using virtual collaboration can also be an important benefit to an organization's clients. Rather than simply drawing on local talent in one area, or forcing their professionals to travel to client locations, as had been done for decades, nowadays professional firms can tap into teams throughout the world to draw on their thought leadership and expertise – at a much lower expense.

And of course, virtual work offers enormous potential savings on real estate, especially in high-cost cities. Some technology companies, such as Stripe,[4] have offered bonuses for employees who relocate to less expensive cities to help minimize commercial real estate expenses. More companies are likely to follow suit and embrace the work-from-anywhere (WFA) trend.

Some leaders see demographics as another driver. "By 2025, 75% of the workforce will be from the millennial generation,"

says Bill McDermott, CEO of ServiceNow, in our conversation. "These employees didn't want to work from office cubicles before COVID-19, and the pandemic only accelerated the need for global businesses and organizations to address this workforce reality. It's essential to give workers choice and make digital businesses work for them; and this reality will persist after we emerge from the pandemic."

That's the good news. Despite those widely cited advantages to working virtually, our research found that many organizations that took the leap into the virtual world were not fully equipped for success. In a 2008 study we conducted of 50 global virtual teams, we found that many virtual teams were not performing to their full potential due to ineffective team leadership, lack of accountability among team members, lack of time to focus on the team, and lack of skills training. In fact, that study found that more than 25% of the virtual teams were not performing up to par, largely because organizations and leaders were approaching work as if the dynamics were the same as working in the same physical location. Even though that study is more than a decade old and was conducted in a dramatically different context, our central finding remains true to this day: far too many companies and leaders have not recognized or appreciated the need to operate differently when at a distance.

The abrupt shift to remote work during the pandemic revealed other challenges. Millions of professionals complained of Zoom/video burnout. Many recognized the widespread challenges managing the blur between work and family life, as well as the increased stress from the health risks and economic crises. The pandemic has been particularly hard on working mothers, who are now spending 71 hours a week working compared to about 50 hours for fathers, according to the Leanin.org study.[5] A 1989 book by sociologist Arlie Hochschild called *The Second Shift*[6] found that women tended to assume most of the household and childcare responsibilities, even though more women were working. Thirty years later, COVID-19 demonstrated that this remains true. As schools shifted to all-remote or hybrid setups, many parents found themselves also trying to be educators, creating tremendous stress and challenges. Yanbing Li, VP of Engineering at Google Cloud, shared a phrase that captured this perfectly. "There's an expression in Silicon Valley," she said, "that with this pandemic, we're all in the same storm, but in different boats." Yanbing is right, that we all have different home setups, family demands, support systems, individual contexts, and financial circumstances. Even though many people are now not commuting to the office or traveling for business, we hear endless stories about people working harder than ever. According to one study,[7] U.S. employees logged 22 million extra hours working during the first months of the pandemic. While technological advancements have made collaboration easier than ever before, people have experienced overload.

Finally, as organizations began planning for after the pandemic recedes, many are focused on what a hybrid solution may look like – a workforce that is partially in the office and partially working remotely. This blended approach presents its own set of challenges. For example, in some company cultures, remote workers feel that their colleagues who are in the office more receive preferential treatment. Other organizations struggle to conduct effective meetings with some people sitting around the conference table and others beaming in on a video screen. As companies shift to virtual work, it will be especially important for leaders to be mindful of potential biases and make sure that they are treating people equitably. In our interviews with senior leaders, we have even seen examples of some organizations creating a new role such as the Head of Remote Work and Culture, and others who are focused on virtual productivity and collaboration. If the current trends continue, these roles may well become ubiquitous.

Our Research on the Virtual Experience During a Pandemic

While researching *Leading at a Distance*, we conducted hundreds of interviews with senior executives. Our goals: to better understand the challenges they were facing, and to assess the future of virtual work within their organizations.

From August to October of 2020, our team partnered with our colleagues at Kincentric (a Spencer Stuart company) to administer several surveys. The first was a 5-item survey administered to 50 top CEOs and CHROs. The survey asked targeted questions about the impact of virtual work on them individually and separately on their organizations, as well as how they are adapting to the current remote environment. We administered a second, similar 5-item survey to broader professionals via a post on LinkedIn, which received approximately 100 responses. Finally, we administered a third survey, which collected data across 11 separate items as well as demographics, and garnered over 500 responses. This last piece of research, what we will call going forward The Virtual Experience survey, was the most robust in terms of capturing people's overall experiences as well as key challenges that they faced, so we will primarily focus on these survey findings from here on out.

These surveys are a slice in time, taken four to six months after companies shifted to remote work. Situational factors – the pandemic and the mass illnesses that resulted, the economic crisis, and the profound upheaval of everyday life – may make some of the findings more challenging to interpret. Nonetheless, our research captures important themes that provide a useful perspective for organizations and leaders as they think through the future of work. In addition, the survey findings were supplemented by more than one hundred interviews and a decade of research and consulting on this topic to provide proven strategies through-out the book.

Key Findings

Let's start with the positive news. Overall, the shift to remote has been generally positive for most people, with 52% of respondents reporting that it has been net positive to them individually and 42% indicating that it has been net positive to the organization. Yes, there is still a percentage of people who fall in the neither net negative nor positive category, but the over-all trend is quite clear. The overall impact of the shift to virtual work on the organization is represented in Figure 1.1, and the impact on the individual in Figure 1.2.

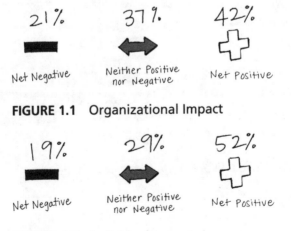

21%   37%   42%

Net Negative   Neither Positive   Net Positive
                nor Negative

FIGURE 1.1   Organizational Impact

19%   29%   52%

Net Negative   Neither Positive   Net Positive
                nor Negative

FIGURE 1.2   Individual Impact

Employee onboarding and personal connection among employees were the most negatively impacted by virtual work, and productivity, technology, work-life balance, and maintaining accountability were the most positively impacted by virtual work (see Figure 1.3).

Virtual work has made detecting and dealing with conflict and developing and mentoring team members most challenging. Using remote working platforms, working across time zones, and ensuring work quality were perceived as least challenging (see Figure 1.4).

	MOST CHALLENGING	NEUTRAL	LEAST CHALLENGING
Using remote working platforms (M Teams, BlueJeans, Zoom, etc.)	8	15	78
Working across time zones	14	19	67
Ensuring work quality	16	25	59
Gaining commitment from team members	20	25	56
Maintaining clear roles and responsibilities	20	26	54
Promoting shared goals	20	34	45
Ability to hold team accountable	22	27	51
Promoting collaboration among team members	27	27	46
Maintaining relationships with team members	32	31	38
Encouraging open and honest communication	34	28	38
Creating a shared vision	34	31	34
Getting and promoting feedback among team members	39	27	34
Building trust virtually	39	27	34
Engaging and motivating team members	40	30	29
Maintaining work-life balance	41	10	49
Mentorship and career development among team members	53	24	24
Detecting dealing with conflict	55	28	16

FIGURE 1.3   Virtual Work: What has been challenging?

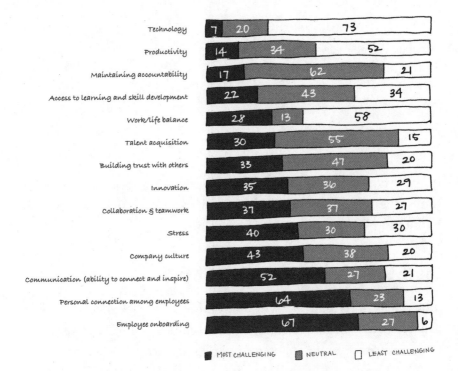

FIGURE 1.4 Virtual Work: Impact on the following factors

Leaders Have Responded with Resilience, Authenticity, and Agility

We are inspired by the countless stories we heard when talking with senior leaders. Perhaps more than ever, leaders have successfully responded with transparency, authenticity, and humility. "People have been more accessible and more informal and fully human," says Kathleen Hogan from Microsoft. eBay's CEO, Jamie Iannone, who joined the company a month after the United States entered lockdown, shared that sentiment. "The world has become more authentic; you see people in their

home environments. We've always said we want people to bring their true selves to work and not create a separation, so now it's happening."

The Hybrid Model May Be Here to Stay

The current situation, while certainly very challenging, has caused many organizations to rethink their future operating models. For example, many companies are now much more open to telecommuting since they have seen evidence that employees are as productive and engaged working virtually as they are in person. Many leaders we spoke to seem to be leaning toward a hybrid model in the future and are already beginning to strategize about some of the challenges with this model. At John Deere Financial, Chief Product Officer Tony Thelen shared that managers quickly realized that three-quarters of their employees were as productive or more productive working from home as they were at the office. As a result, Deere is exploring hybrid working models.

At many companies, 10% to 20% of employees say they never want to come back to the office, 10% to 20% prefer to come back full time, and the rest hope for a flexible approach. "People jump to the conclusion that Work from Home is the best model, but I'm not convinced," says one global 100 CHRO.

Productivity Has Not Been Negatively Impacted

When people consider remote work, perhaps the number one concern that we hear is the idea that people will be less productive if they are not in the office. And how can leaders hold people accountable, some think, if they are not working typical hours and they don't have a clear sense of what people are working on? Won't they goof off? The good news is that 52% of respondents in our survey indicated that productivity has been positively impacted by virtual work, and only 14% said that productivity has been negatively impacted. Natalie Atwood, senior vice president of People at HealthEquity recalls the reaction among her company's leadership. "We have been wowed by the performance of our team members working from home. We were not dead set against remote work before, but now we are much more open to it."

Technology and Time Zone Differences are No Longer Barriers

In our 2008 research on virtual work, we found that overcoming time zone differences and properly leveraging technology were significant challenges. However, today, 73% of respondents in our Virtual Experience survey found that technology has had a positive impact on remote work. Of course, advancements in technology have contributed to this favorable perception, but people have also had to adjust to using technology in different ways. People are more comfortable using videoconferencing, messaging and collaboration platforms, and even social media to stay engaged with colleagues and customers. The current environment has forced people to accept and leverage technology in new and different ways. Some people, however, responded more negatively, reporting that their organizations did not have adequate training on how to leverage technology to support their work.

Work-Life Balance Is a Net Positive

Our research also shows that work-life balance is a net positive for most people (58%), which was the second-highest-rated dimension in terms of positivity. Many people feel happy about skipping their long commutes and having more flexible hours, as well as seeing their families. In addition, few people are traveling for business due to the pandemic, which has also helped with work-life balance. However, we do recognize that this has not been a net positive for everyone: 28% indicated that it has been a net negative and 13% said net neutral. During the first weeks of the crisis, David Zaslav, the CEO of media company Discovery Inc., shared that he found himself on Zoom calls from 6 a.m. to 8 p.m. with few breaks. The stressful, desk-bound lifestyle wasn't sustainable for a leader like David who fed off of – and gave energy to – others he worked with in his intensive collaborative management style. So David, a former collegiate tennis player who was quarantining at his home in eastern Long Island, called a nearby club and asked if he could hire a pro for a one-hour daily hitting session. When we spoke with him, he'd had 80 one-hour hits in 80 days. "It's been great for stress and to keep me able to provide the engaged leadership our global team needs," he said. "And I'm going to come out of this playing tennis as well as I have in years!"

More Opportunities for Learning and Development

Many employees working from home had greater access to online training, and 34% of our survey respondents reported that working remotely has been a net positive for learning and skill development. Many of our clients have adjusted their learning strategies and implemented virtual offerings, which gives more people greater access to these learning experiences. As one example, when Starbucks sent its 58,000 employees[8] in China home, it continued to pay them and suggested they take online courses through Starbucks China University. Some organizations have realized that it is possible to deliver engaging and impactful learning opportunities in the virtual environment. And some, like Rosie Allan, senior director of Talent Management, Learning and Culture at FINRA, says they are seeing that participation levels in learning and development programs have increased as people shifted to home.

While these trends are generally good news, let's look at some of the less positive news.

Burnout Is Real

Our Virtual Experience survey data supports what so many professionals have been discussing: people are experiencing significant levels of burnout. There is less separation between work and family life, especially with many children home from school. In many regions, everyone in the family is remote and going through things together, which puts additional pressure on working parents. Forty percent of respondents in our survey indicated that stress has increased, causing their overall wellness to have been negatively impacted. People are working longer hours, often using time after dinner to attack the backlog of emails from back-to-back videoconferences during the day or to make progress on other important responsibilities. Having children at home can increase stress and magnify the responsibilities, causing burnout. In addition, people are not taking vacations or much time off, perhaps due to the pandemic or a concern about job security.

Middle Managers Aren't the Only Ones Facing Burnout

We've already explored some of the ways the shift to virtual work has increased the workload, working hours, and stress levels of many workers – and been especially punishing for women and working parents. But our research also makes clear that the rapid shift to a virtual setting has negatively impacted CEOs more than non-CEO survey respondents (see Figure 1.5, which comes from our LinkedIn survey). From our discussions with executives, this is happening because CEOs and other senior leaders are investing time to overcommunicate to employees and external stakeholders during this time of great stress and ambiguity. This has required endless meetings, COVID-19 task forces, internal town halls, and other forums to stay connected and engaged with stakeholders. Top executives at a major omnichannel retailer worry that too much time is spent in meetings with the same 20 colleagues and fear they are missing the

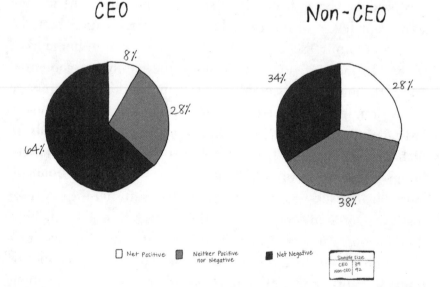

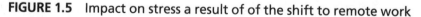

FIGURE 1.5   Impact on stress a result of of the shift to remote work

short- and long-term benefits of serendipitous interactions. The CEO of a US-based retailer argued that organization-wide, people are spending far too much time talking to each other through computer screens in a frequency and mode of communication that is not sustainable.

People Miss the Personal Connection with Colleagues

Perhaps not surprisingly, 64% of people surveyed indicated that personal connections with colleagues have been negatively impacted. The shift to remote, coupled with the global pandemic, has resulted in greater feelings of isolation. "One of the groups that is most challenged by the COVID situation is Generation Z," according to Tina Jones, senior vice president for Global Human Resources at Cadence Design Systems. "Work was meant to be an important piece of their social fabric. The inability to be with that community – to see people in person during and after work – is a real loss."

Innovation Is at Risk

Only 29% of respondents indicated that innovation has been positively impacted, 36% said innovation is neutral, and 35% said it has been a net negative. While some companies have adapted to the virtual environment and have leveraged tools to foster innovation, others have not had such a positive experience. At Discovery Inc., producers have shot over 1,500 hours of programming on iPhones and Go Pros at a fraction of what they ordinarily spend to produce content. "One has been nominated for an Emmy," says David Zaslav, the CEO. "We've had kids of our talent shooting on iPhones." Is this a short-term pandemic-only phenomenon? "That is the question for us! Is this new content, in which we made up for a diminution of production excellence with total authenticity, being loved now and only in this moment? When this is over, will this be a new genre of reality programming? Personally, I think there is a sustainable creative element of this – sharing content in your real world, not in the studio."

It may be too early to form a conclusion about the impact of remote work on innovation. Many studies have shown that virtual collaboration fosters innovation, due in part to increased anonymity and the use of technology to brainstorm. Therefore, it is possible that the current environment, where many organizations had to rapidly shift their business strategy from investments in growth to cost cutting, could also be skewing these early findings. Some organizations that believe in the power of technology to innovate leverage technologies like MURAL and Miro to collaborate in real time with colleagues.

Organizations Are Struggling with Remote Onboarding

Employee onboarding has been a significant challenge according to our survey findings, with 67% of respondents saying that it has been negatively impacted. Given that many people find it difficult to build relationships virtually, think about how hard it may be for a new employee to feel welcome and part of a broader team. While many organizations have transformed their onboarding programs for a virtual setting, we are still hearing that nothing truly replaces those in-person meetings with colleagues. In a later chapter, we will share some examples and tips on how organizations can maximize virtual onboarding.

One company experiencing that onboarding challenge is Goldman Sachs. "We just hired 2,700 new people from undergrad; they've just started," Goldman's CEO David Solomon, told us during the summer of 2020. "We're trying all sorts of things to connect them. But it's a different experience for them compared to working from the office and getting the hands-on training that is the hallmark of our firm." Goldman is the epitome of the "apprenticeship" culture – a company that hires large numbers of entry-level professionals and invests significant resources in training them. This culture creates special challenges when working virtually (something we'll address in greater detail in Chapter 10).

As leaders reflect on the positives and negatives of leading through the pandemic, some see truth in the old maxim that crisis presents an opportunity. Goldman's CEO is one example of that. David, who led Goldman's investment banking division before succeeding Lloyd Blankfein as CEO in October 2018, had been in the role fewer than 18 months when the pandemic rattled global markets and forced all the big banks to shift to remote work. For financial institutions, which must worry more than most companies about data security and regulatory requirements ("this call is on a recorded line"), the shift required quickly building remote infrastructure; the bank even had to ship desk phones to several thousand employees to ensure they had the necessary telephonic capabilities at home. As a newer CEO, David saw the pandemic as a chance to demonstrate his competence. "As a CEO, I felt a responsibility to demonstrate leadership," he said. "That's one of the reasons why I went into the office, to show up and be present."

The Bottom Line

- Long before COVID-19, companies were starting to embrace remote work to gain advantages in the war for talent, in cost, and in increased diversity; because it gave them the ability to take advantage of trends in technology and globalization; and because it allowed them to be closer to customers.

- Our research shows that 52% of executives believe the shift to remote work has been positive for organizations, and 42% believe it's been positive for them as individuals. Productivity has held steady or increased even as work-life balance has shifted positively.

- A hybrid model, in which workers alternate between days at home and days in the office, seems likely to be the predominant model in the future. Employees, who have had a taste of the increased flexibility from working remotely, eliminating daily commuting and avoiding nonessential business travel, do not want to go all the way back. However, leaders must deal with the challenges of the hybrid model, which can create problems with inclusion and a perceived lack of equity, challenges for onboarding, and take a toll on employee relationships and corporate culture over time.

Notes

1 Charles Handy, "Trust and the Virtual Organization," *Harvard Business Review*, May–June 1995, https://hbr.org/1995/05/trust-and-the-virtual-organization.

2 Matthew Fox, "Zoom overtakes Exxon Mobil in market value amid COVID-19 pandemic," *Business Insider*, October 29, 2020, www.businessinsider.com/zoom-exxon-mobil-overtakes-market-value-stock-price-covid19-pandemic-2020-10.

3 Sarah Coury et al., "Women in the Workplace," McKinsey & Company, September 30, 2020, www.mckinsey.com/featured-insights/diversity-and-inclusion/women-in-the-workplace#.

4 Avery Hartmans, "Stripe is reportedly cutting pay for employees who leave Seattle, New York, or the Bay Area, but will also provide a $20,000 incentive to move," *Business*

Insider, September 16, 2020, www.businessinsider.com/stripe-cuts-pay-offers-bonuses-to-employees-who-relocate-report-2020-9.

5 "Women are maxing out and burning out during COVID-19," Leanin.org, May 7, 2020, https://leanin.org/article/womens-workload-and-burnout.

6 Robert Kuttmer, "She Minds the Child, He Minds the Dog," *New York Times,* June 25, 1989, www.nytimes.com/1989/06/25/books/she-minds-the-child-he-minds-the-dog.html.

7 Jo Craven McGinty, "With No Commute, Americans Simply Worked More During Coronavirus," *Wall Street Journal,* October 30, 2020, www.wsj.com/articles/with-no-commute-americans-simply-worked-more-during-coronavirus-11604050200.

8 Linda Dahlstrom and Marianne Duong, "One global company's steps to navigate COVID-19 in China – and the lessons learned," Starbucks Stories & News (blog), March 5, 2020, https://stories.starbucks.com/stories/2020/one-global-companys-bold-steps-to-navigate-covid-19-in-china-and-the-lessons-learned/.

2

No Trust = No Team: The Formula for Building Cohesive Relationships Virtually

We were recently working with a global virtual tech team with members in London, New York, and Chicago. People within each of these locations worked together well, but they did not often include team members from other locations. As a result, silos formed. Not surprisingly, the silos and lack of information sharing were impacting team performance. Morale was low, decision-making was slow, and things were getting bogged down.

Happily, there are ways to break down the silos, build trust, and increase collaboration. It starts with the chicken-and-egg question. That is, do high-performing teams create trust, or does trust create high-performing teams?

Our previous global study on virtual collaboration found that top-performing virtual teams report higher levels of trust than teams that are less successful. This research confirms what we have learned from many years of experience with virtual teams: Trust is a foundational ingredient and *precondition* for their success.

Despite the importance of trust in virtual collaboration, building trust can be quite difficult. Our Virtual Experience survey reinforced this, with 39% of respondents reporting that trust is a challenge virtually. Many organizations do not appreciate how working remotely makes it more difficult to build strong relationships. Physical distance makes it harder to find shared experiences that human beings use to help forge personal relationships that help build trust.

Co-located teams see each other regularly and have an ongoing series of interactions. Virtual teams must rely heavily on task-based trust, which is the belief that team members will do their job. Accountability, then, is at the center of the relationship. Of course, task-based trust does not happen on its own, either. It must be developed, and that occurs when virtual team members are responsive, follow through on commitments, and take responsibility for results.

Warning Signs of Low Trust

△! WARNING
   Signs of Low Trust

When trust is low in a virtual team, members will struggle to be successful. There are a few warning signs of low trust that everyone should watch out for:

- **Team members not referring to themselves as "we," focusing instead on their personal needs and agendas.** If team members do not feel they are getting the support they need, or everyone is focused on their own needs, it's not an environment that's conducive to trust.

- **Every conversation is strictly business.** Intimacy is one of the essential elements for building trust, and it requires more effort when working from a distance. Your team members don't have to know every detail of each other's lives, but they should know something about their families and what's important to them. When one member of a high-performing virtual team sent a gift certificate on behalf of the entire team for two nights of doggie day care to another member who had just gotten a puppy for her birthday, it spoke volumes about personal knowledge and went a long way to build trust. If you can find common ground when it comes to things like fitness, kids, geopolitics, or favorite television shows, it is far easier to reach an understanding when it counts. Scheduling regular team-building activities, which for virtual teams are becoming more creative through technology, is much more important since virtual teams do not typically interact outside of a work context.

- **Silos developing among subgroups.** Hosting regular team meetings, brainstorming sessions, and status updates in which everyone participates can help team members see how their individual contributions fit into the big picture and break down silos. Whenever possible, make the effort to connect with your virtual team on video where you can see facial expressions and members' remote workspaces, which lets you read and acknowledge their environments. Good communication helps team members ensure that everyone is accountable and that no one person is being forced to pick up the slack.

- **Micromanagement**. Excessive oversight suggests that people do not trust others to follow through on commitments. Within virtual teams, there is a temptation for leaders to check in more often because they don't see their team members face to face. But there is a difference between checking in to see if someone needs support and constantly monitoring their progress. When team members feel like they are being watched all the time, or, even worse, nagged, they will rightly conclude that their leader does not trust them. Virtual leaders need to work with each team member to find out just how much management they need to do their work effectively. Since this will vary from person to person and project to project, leaders must work to build these relationships and tailor their management and communications styles to each member of the team.

- **Conflicts not being resolved.** Unresolved conflicts cause lingering resentment or even hostility. When someone makes a misstep or does something aggravating, do your team members talk about it to everyone except that person? If so, that's a sign of a potentially toxic environment. It is impossible to be trustful if you are looking over your shoulder wondering if you will be the next target. Although managing conflict can be challenging, taking the time to air out disagreements can diffuse the tension. While the underlying issues may not be solved, simply knowing that they are being heard can help get past disagreements and refocus the team.

- **Playing the blame game.** If people point the finger the other way and no one takes accountability (or is held accountable) for their actions, it is a sure sign your team suffers from a lack of trust. When teams are built upon mutual trust, people should feel free to have open and honest communication about what went wrong and how to fix it. Team members who refuse to take accountability when things go wrong are more concerned with their own survival than with the team's success. Effective leaders find ways to reset expectations and make sure that everyone understands why their tasks are valuable to the team.

- **The Superhero phenomenon.** Do some team members consistently try to take on *too much* themselves and then look for the affirmation of being a superhero? This can signal a lack of trust. Reliability is an important component of trust, one that can only be built over time. In high-performing teams each member pulls his or her weight. Within virtual teams, the instinct for some to take on additional work often begins from a good place, but it can quickly turn into resentment if a team member feels that others aren't doing their part. Conversely, team members who feel like other people do not trust them to do their jobs quickly become frustrated over not having an opportunity to prove they can make valuable contributions to the team.

Be cognizant of these warning signs and better understand what high and low trust look like when working virtually. Here are some examples of high trust versus low trust environments.

Examples of Low Trust

Poor communication	"You can tell Greg about the new product specification if you want. I'm not doing it. He never told me about the change in our rebate policy last week."
Culture of blame	"I should have never trusted Jennifer. She blamed me for the delay with the report when it was her who passed it late to me!"
Unresolved conflicts; negativity	"How can we be productive as a team if Deb and Kyle avoid interacting with each other?"
Lack of reliability	"Ann said she'd send me the sales data book by noon. Well, it's 4 p.m., and I haven't heard from her. It's always this way."
Silos, not "we"	"I rarely interact with the IT guys on the team; they keep to themselves, laugh at their private jokes, and only help each other."

Examples of High Trust

Transparency	"I feel that team leader was up front about the quality control issue."
Relationship	"Mary takes time to listen, even when we run against a tight deadline. I am comfortable sharing ideas and concerns with her."
Credibility	"Tim is doing a good job coordinating the project action plan. I always know what is expected of me and of others."
Reliability	"My teammates have my back. I can rely on their hard work to make the project happen."
Collaboration	"We hit rough patches sometimes, but we manage to bridge our differences and work together."

Building Trust in a Virtual Team:
The Credibility Factor

If you have ever worked with someone you did not trust, you know how difficult and unpleasant it is to get anything done. Trust is the binding agent that holds all relationships together; without it, relationships and teams disintegrate quickly. Virtual teams can be more susceptible to trust issues simply because they do not have the same opportunities for interaction as teams that are located under one roof. Trust consists of four elements that develop through a series of interactions over time:[1]

1. **Reliability:** Consistent behavior shows that people can depend on one another. Example: A co-worker delivers on a promise to meet a tight deadline, and the client is thrilled.

2. **Intimacy:** Close, familiar, and authentic behavior creates affection between team members. Example: A few days later, she tells a funny story about her four-year-old daughter.

3. **Orientation:** The extent to which others believe you care about their concerns. Example: A few weeks later, she fills in for a colleague who is dealing with a family crisis.

4. **Credibility:** The quality of being believable, truthful, and a source of expertise or authority. Example: A few months later, she offers her expertise and makes recommendations on how to handle a situation the team has not encountered before.

Let's take a closer look at the role credibility plays when building trust in a virtual team.

If team members believe someone is selectively disclosing information or putting a positive spin on the facts in order to gain support, his or her credibility will suffer. People demonstrate credibility through credentials, words, and actions. Being perceived as credible is not only a matter of what someone says, but how they say it and how consistent their actions are with their words.

Within a virtual team, it can be more difficult to get to know other team members. Casual conversations are less frequent, and context is frequently lost through email, Slack, or even phone conversations. When someone has recently joined a team or is new to a leadership role, team members may not know much about them. When a leader spends intentional time up front with new members of the team, to get to know their past experiences, goals and aspirations, and personal stories, it builds credibility.

Decision-making can also be less transparent within a virtual team. Leaders may make decisions in silos, without understanding how their actions may impact someone in another location. Team members who only hear the final decision may believe it was made hastily or without consideration, when in fact it just as easily may have followed a rigorous process they had not observed. They may perceive the leader as someone who makes snap judgments, rather than adhering to best practices.

Unless virtual leaders and team members have established credibility, they will never have the level of trust required to motivate and inspire their team and maintain high levels of productivity.

As a leader, here are tips for enhancing trust in virtual teams:

- **Provide opportunities to build relationships.** If possible, new virtual teams should meet face to face at least once within the first few months.

- **Offer professional networking opportunities for team members to share their capabilities.** Hosting "lunch and learn" sessions where team members take turns presenting on a topic where they have expertise can improve their credibility and make others more likely to consult them when they need help. These don't have to be on topics related to the business. One team had a monthly Zoom session presenting on "sharing your unknown talent," and reports are that after a colleague gave a detailed presentation on gemology, his stature within the group skyrocketed.

- **Speak the truth.** Respond to questions in an honest and complete manner to deliver clarity and transparency. Be balanced – communicate the positive aspects as well as the downsides – when making a proposal. Avoid withholding information that may weaken your position but that others would find useful when deciding.

- **Highlight successes.** A proven track record of success is one of the best indicators of credibility. Encourage team members to share their wins through email, during meetings, or social media pages when appropriate. One highly distributed team created a punchy, well-designed weekly news roundup of the extended team's wins. But rather than just list the success stories, they put them in the context of external market developments, and always did so with the engaging lines "What you need to know," and "Why it matters."

- **Encourage and role-model transparency.** Emphasize the importance and show the power of being open and honest. Invite team members to regularly share their challenges as well as their successes, whether during meetings or by posting them in an internal forum and opening them up for discussion. Lead by example to give permission to others to do the same. Whenever possible, make project timelines, agreements, and processes fully transparent. Recognize that employees increasingly view transparency as something to which they're entitled. A major omni-channel retail CHRO shared in our interview with him that the desire [or demand] for transparency currently exceeds any previous expectations.

- **Admit when you don't know something.** Few things are a bigger turn off than a know-it-all. Rather than pretending to know everything, or even if you do, virtual leaders should set an example by being vulnerable, genuinely soliciting the input of others, and always admitting, even advertising, what they don't know. Leaders should consult other colleagues and experts for information and encourage team members to do the same. Aaron Walters, chairman and CEO of the women's retailer Altar'd State, told us that we "opened up [our] leadership team's visibility and vulnerability, and it has had a massive impact. [We] were rated 83 out of 100 in the Great Places to Work Survey and now [we] are over 90, in a pandemic."

Building trust within a virtual team takes time and focus, but it is worth the effort. In a study of 600 virtual team members, 81% reported that building rapport and trust was the greatest personal challenge they faced. Our own research on virtual teams shows that trust is one of the most important factors distinguishing top-performing teams from less successful ones. The ability to foster trust within a team is a skill that leaders can develop through training and development. For virtual teams to be successful, team members need to have confidence in one another's credibility. Remote workers are not afforded the same level of networking as in-office teams, so avoid taking the nature of trust for granted.

Trust is built naturally among teams that interact in person each day, but it takes more effort to develop among teams that rarely (if ever) meet face to face. Virtual leaders need to create an environment that fosters trust. When trust breaks down, however, they will struggle to be productive.

The Bottom Line

- Trust is a prerequisite for virtual team success, but it is harder to build virtually: 39% of executives report experiencing challenges in building trust in a remote environment. Building task-based trust early on is important for virtual teams.

- Leaders can create a trusting environment through open, frequent, and transparent communication; by encouraging team members to share aspects of their personal lives to build intimacy; and by admitting when they don't know something.

- Signs of low virtual trust include poor communication, a culture of blame, unresolved conflicts, a lack of follow though, silos, and an "I" orientation instead of a "we" orientation.

Note

1 Trusted Advisor Associates LLC, "Understanding the Trust Equation," accessed December 1, 2020, https://trustedadvisor. com/why-trust-matters/understanding-trust/understanding- the-trust-equation.

3

What Does Good Look Like? Profile of High-Performing Virtual Teams

Not every organization uses virtual teams to their full potential. In our previous study of virtual teams, we discovered that more than a quarter (27%) were not "fully performing." Many organizations simply recycled the same guidelines they were using for their co-located teams and hoped for the best. And frankly, that system does not work.

This chapter explores what factors make virtual teams perform successfully and outlines key pitfalls for virtual collaboration. The next chapter outlines how to maximize virtual team performance and overcome performance plateaus.

We are regularly asked these kinds of questions: *What team size is optimal? Do cross-functional teams have more challenges? How often should virtual teams meet face to face?* These and similar questions led to our research study on virtual team effectiveness, in which we collected data to provide practical, research-based recommendations to leaders and managers. We found that the characteristics of high-performing virtual teams fell into three categories: team composition, communication and training, and leadership. Among teams that were most successful, strong leadership was a common thread.

Composition	Communication and Training	Leadership
• Stable and consistent membership. • Fewer team members (37% of teams with 13+ members rated themselves as less effective). • Members are from the same function. • Members are on fewer teams. • Longer tenure (teams working together for 3+ years performed best).	• Host an in-person kickoff meeting with in the first 90 days. • Host weekly meetings (67% of high-performing teams meet at least once a week). • Use technology, including video conferencing. • Teams that had 4+ training sessions performed best.	• Team leaders can build collaboration virtually. • The most successful leaders have team members who report directly to them.

Team Composition

Decisions about team size and membership are critical to the success of virtual teams.

Stable Team Membership

Top-performing teams in our study had a core group whose membership did not fluctuate frequently. On less effective teams, however, members were frequently added and removed. For example, one of the less effective virtual teams saw its membership changed on a monthly basis. This caused confusion about who was on the team and led to role ambiguity. With less frequent changes in membership, high-performing teams had greater stability and more time for members to build relationships.

Fewer Team Members

The less effective teams in our study were disproportionately larger. For example, 37% of low-performing teams had 13 or more members, compared to just 24% of the top-performing teams. The bottom line is that when geographically distributed teams become too large, it is more difficult for their members to collaborate effectively.

Let's look at a high-performing virtual team that effectively managed team membership. Team SolveIT is a global information technology team with 10 members each in a different location. The organization had previously formed larger teams so that employees would not be left out even if they did not have a clear role. Some of these team members never even participated on projects. To avoid creating a team that was too large, the leader decided to keep the core team small, but formed advisory groups, which acted as collaborators beyond the core members. This proved to be beneficial in that it provided the team with additional resources when they were needed while keeping people engaged with clear roles on the team.

Team Members Are from the Same Function

Most of the high-performing teams in our study were not cross-functional, while most lower-performing teams were. In a virtual environment, the complexities that come with being a cross-functional team can impact performance. Cross-functional teams are especially susceptible to problems caused by lack of accountability since they operate in a matrix structure where team leaders may not have formal authority.

Team Members Belong to Fewer Teams

Forty-two percent of members of low-performing teams reported that a key challenge was finding the time to participate on a given team because they were spread so thin across multiple teams. During our interviews with members of the low-performing teams, we learned that people are frequently invited to participate on a team even if they will not have a specific role. This was often done with the best intentions, so that team members did not feel left out. In many situations, team membership is outside of one's normal job requirements. For example, people may be invited to join special task forces to investigate a customer problem or provide recommendations. Yet this extra work is not necessarily part of their day-to-day responsibilities. When people end up on too many virtual teams, they cannot fulfill all their day-to-day obligations as well as meet their team deadlines.

Longer Tenure as a Team

Teams that have existed for more than three years performed better than those that have not. By working together over time, long-tenured teams were able to successfully implement processes that support teamwork and communication. For example,

R&D teams with long tenure and membership stability have established team practices that lead to success over time. The winning factor here is experience. Our recent Virtual Experience survey findings further reinforce the importance of team tenure on performance, as it was once again identified as a key driver of virtual team effectiveness.

Communication and Training

Although technology is the foundation that enables effective virtual collaboration, in no way does it guarantee successful virtual teamwork. Success requires using technologies to communicate effectively. Even in a time of necessary remote work, it is preferable to communicate *without* technology at times.

Face-to-Face Meetings

Our study found that virtual teams that held an initial face-to-face meeting within the first 90 days of coming together performed better than those who never met face to face. Bottom line: face-to-face meetings are an investment that pays off. Bringing team members together to clarify goals and roles and to get to know one another is beneficial. Yet, for various reasons, it is not always possible to hold an in-person kickoff meeting. It may not be worth the time and cost to arrange a face-to-face kickoff meeting if the virtual team has been assembled to deal with a short-term problem. In such instances, we recommend a series of videoconferences to accomplish the same objectives. And while it is true that virtual teams can find ways to make up for the lack of face-to-face interaction, in-person meetings do lead to better performance.

Effective "V-meetings"

A global operations team would meet via teleconference on a weekly basis. The team had a formal leader but rotated the role of meeting facilitator. The assigned facilitator was responsible for sending out a draft agenda in advance of the one-hour call to solicit team member input to help prioritize agenda items. One team member recalled, "Our virtual meetings are highly efficient since we manage our time well. We do not waste a ton of time providing basic updates to one another, as we can do this via email."

In contrast, a global technology team met weekly via one-hour teleconferences. In this case, the team leader led each meeting and did not solicit input from team members regarding agenda items in advance. Instead, at the beginning of each meeting, everyone on the call would waste time crafting the agenda. Next people provided basic updates, which did not change significantly week to week. As a result, many team members did not pay attention. Clearly, this team would have benefited from better v-meeting management, which we discuss in Chapter 6 on how to lead effective virtual meetings.

Well-Leveraged Technology

High-performing teams were more likely to report that they had technology that helped them work together. Low-performing teams were more likely to suffer from technology overload and were less likely to match technology to the task. For example, many high-performing teams use webinars and collaborative technologies for brainstorming and decision-making, while lower-performing teams rely more heavily on email. In some cases, low-performing teams also reported experiencing more technology problems and indicated that they lacked appropriate training. We found that technology should be viewed as a catalyst for virtual team performance improvement, not a remedy. In other words, simply using the technology just because you have it will not immediately solve your virtual team problems. If you are the leader and are putting a virtual team together, take responsibility to launch the team with technology support and encourage a launch meeting on team protocols. This increases the odds that the team will use the practices that are the hallmarks of high-performing teams.

Skill Development

Virtual teams that had more than four team development sessions performed significantly better than those who did not. Forty-five percent of those in the study said that the top skill development needs for those working in virtual teams are communication and interpersonal skills, followed by collaboration skills.

We found that many organizations launch virtual teams without providing the necessary training to support them. Let's say a virtual team comes together for the first time on a project, but they are not trained properly in how to communicate and collaborate with one another. Deficiencies in those skills snowball in a virtual setting where team members need to adapt their style and approach in order to remain productive. You must carefully assess employees you are considering for virtual teams, make sure you select those who have the appropriate skill sets, and ensure that those selected have the necessary training to be successful.

We recommend collecting data to assess the areas that are barriers for the team before providing generic training. Targeted training is more effective and will provide a better return on investment for the organization.

Having the teams work on assignments in between sessions helps create momentum and continuity. It also provides opportunities for teams to collaborate on real-world business issues, which helps reinforce the skills taught in training sessions. Jane Datta, CHRO at NASA, echoes the importance of skill development and ongoing learning related to real business issues. "One breakthrough was really focusing on our supervisors," she told us. "They are having to adjust for their own sakes and how they operate with their teams. We've done one-hour Friday virtual sessions with speakers, panelists, and discussions about how to make connections with your team, how to help employees who are concerned or anxious, how to manage diversity, and other important topics. It's not that we have all the answers, but we've found that providing a forum so that they can leverage each other and bring that community together all really helps, and we have high attendance."

Leadership and Management

Not surprisingly, leadership plays a major role in virtual team performance. Many of the low-performing teams in our study had ineffective leaders. Top-performing leaders balance the people-oriented and execution-oriented responsibilities associated with managing virtual teams.

The methods used by the high-performing teams we have discussed here should be considered when forming or reorganizing virtual teams. In most cases, companies can and should control factors such as team size and skill development for virtual team members. If organizations want their virtual teams to be best-in-class, it is important that they understand what factors must come together to create that distinction – and to implement them early on.

Common Problems That Hurt Virtual Team Performance

Our study also identified factors that hurt the performance of virtual teams, as detailed in the following sections.

Who Is Doing What? How Do We Shift Work as Priorities Evolve?

As with any team, virtual or co-located, a lack of clear goals and priorities will inhibit team performance. And because it is tougher to communicate with team members who are geographically distributed, this can be an even bigger problem for virtual teams. One virtual team member stated, "While our goals are very clear, they change so frequently, which leads to ambiguity." The most effective virtual teams reassess goals as priorities shift over time. Teams that do this effectively are usually those with the best leaders.

Lack of Clear Roles Among Team Members

In virtual teams, it is important for team members to clearly understand their roles. A poorly designed accountability structure can have a huge impact on virtual teams. For example, if a global product development team is working virtually, it would not be efficient for team members in Asia to have to wait to check on how to proceed on a given initiative with team members in New York, who start their business day much later. What would work best is if the team members in Asia have the authority to make decisions based on their own scope of work. Designing an effective accountability structure minimizes delays and inefficiencies that are common when working virtually.

One global information technology team developed a great way to communicate team member roles. They created a virtual team playbook, which provided background on each team member and clearly laid out roles. When questions arose during complex projects, team members had an easy way to identify who to go to.

A Lack of Engagement

Many virtual team members in our study reported a lack of engagement that resulted from not feeling challenged. It can be difficult to assess individual team members' levels of engagement because they are in different locations and rarely have face-to-face interactions. To avoid this common problem, leaders should proactively look for signs of disengagement.

For example, are all team members contributing to conversations and projects? Are they attending and actively participating in team meetings? Are team members motivated to take on new work or are they feeling overwhelmed? Are people working well together or is there frequent and unproductive team conflict?

One global team we worked with experienced this very problem. Several of the team's members reported feelings of isolation and a lack of connectivity with others on the team. In a virtual setting, this is very common. People easily become bored and "check out" because there is a lack of dynamic face-to-face interaction and because there are more distractions.

Lack of Accountability

When no one is willing to admit mistakes or take responsibility for their actions, it is difficult for a team to function effectively. It is also difficult to have open and honest conversations about what is going wrong and how to fix it. When team members are more concerned about protecting themselves rather than helping their peers succeed, it's a warning sign of dysfunction in the team. Self-preservation could take several forms: withholding information, not involving others in decisions, refusing to help others, avoiding responsibility, bashing other team members behind their backs, and actively undermining them to make them look bad. This creates an environment that erodes relationships and makes it difficult to work collaboratively toward accomplishing key goals.

Micromanaging

A manager who constantly checks in to make sure everyone is doing their job might appear helpful, but it also indicates a lack of confidence in others. In any case, the outcome isn't likely to be good. Either their lack of confidence is well-founded and the micromanager ends up supporting a team member who can't perform at the appropriate level, or they wind up frustrating an otherwise capable employee who will likely head for the door rather than deal with constant oversight.

Conflict Avoidance

Conflict often has a negative connotation, but it is a natural and healthy aspect of any team environment. Team members will not always agree with one another, nor should they. Diversity of opinion helps teams identify new ways of looking at problems and alternative methods for solving them. Sometimes those differences can lead to tension, but when team members trust and respect one another, these conflicts are more likely to be resolved positively to produce mutually beneficial outcomes.

Given the importance of conflict management, it is disconcerting that detecting and managing conflict was the top-rated challenge (55%) in our Virtual Experience survey. This may be due, at least in part, to the idea that conflict is harder to detect virtually. Also, if people do not have a solid, trusting relationship with a colleague, they are much less likely to proactively address potential conflict. This means that leaders need to be more attentive to helping people manage conflict.

The RAMP Model

Based on our global study of what differentiates top-performing virtual teams, our experiences working directly with virtual teams, and the lessons we learned about why virtual teams fail, we developed the RAMP model. This model is designed to serve as a roadmap for virtual teams and their leaders, and it provides practical steps to accelerate performance. The model is comprised of four components that are critical to virtual team success (see Figure 3.1).

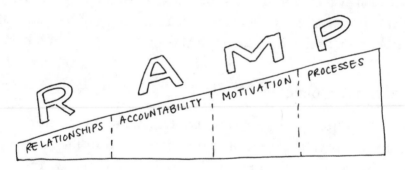

FIGURE 3.1

Relationships

Two of the top drivers of virtual team performance fall under the dimension of relationships. Specifically, maintaining relationships with team members and promoting collaboration among team members are critical to virtual team performance. The most successful virtual teams find ways to collaborate effectively and work together to achieve their collective goals. Our research indicates that teams that focus solely on execution without attending to interpersonal relationships are not nearly as effective.

Accountability

The ability to hold team members accountable is also an important driver of team effectiveness. What does a culture of accountability look like in virtual teams? Those that get accountability right follow through on commitments. These teams tolerate honest mistakes, and when problems arise, members engage in creative problem-solving rather than rationalizing and justifying shortfalls. In addition, everyone takes full responsibility for their actions and outcomes – and people count on one another rather than trying to avoid blame. Some virtual teams operate like self-managed work teams (SMWTs), or self-directed teams, where members collaborate and hold one another accountable for meeting commitments. For example, SMWTs do not have formal leaders. Instead, team members rotate in and out of the leadership position depending on the project.

Motivation

A fundamental part of motivating virtual teams is the ability to inspire team members. This means creating purpose and meaning for your work to motivate the team. Given that some virtual teams operate like SMWTs, it is also sometimes important for virtual team members to motivate one another.

Process

Finally, to collaborate effectively, members of top-performing teams ensure they have a good understanding of one another's roles and responsibilities and that the team has clearly defined objectives. They trust one another to achieve objectives and have a process in place to communicate and share work.

In the next chapter, we will cover strategies to RAMP up your virtual team's performance.

The Bottom Line

- High-performing virtual teams have stable and consistent membership, long-tenured members, and a team size of 13 or fewer. They know when and how to best leverage technology to support the team. Further, they are led by leaders and managers who set clear roles and goals, ensure accountability, and lead with empowerment to increase engagement.

- If your team cannot meet in person for a kickoff or important event, use a series of short virtual meetings to replicate what would occur in person.

- High-performing teams are effective in all dimensions of the RAMP model, which emphasizes **Relationships**, **Accountability**, **Motivation**, and **Processes**, to enhance effectiveness.

4

How to RAMP Up Your Virtual Team's Performance: A Blueprint for Success

The previous chapter introduced the RAMP model of virtual team effectiveness. This chapter provides practical tips and guidelines to bring this to life with your virtual team.

Before we dive in, let's share a quick case study of how the RAMP model can be used to accelerate virtual team performance. We worked with a senior executive of a global professional services firm who had realized that several of their virtual teams were having significant performance issues. Most team members were new to virtual work. We conducted live interviews and a survey to gather feedback on what was working well – and what wasn't – among the four RAMP dimensions. We found the greatest weaknesses in Motivation and Processes: the leaders were not effectively inspiring their teams, nor were they well-organized to problem-solve or make decisions. They made up for those weaknesses by being strong in Relationships and Accountability. The team members were well-networked, solution-oriented, and enjoyed working together, so we tried to elevate the other dimensions to bring the team toward success. The leaders and team members had the rapport needed, so we put the leaders through targeted skill-building training on how to set a common purpose and goal for their groups. With clearer objectives, including both specific metrics and higher-level motivators, the leaders were able to thoughtfully restructure their teams and clarify roles.

Our work with this client made clear that uninspired and uncertain employees, as talented as they may be, do not make for a strong team. When your team is virtual, the way in which you tackle and give airtime to Relationships, Accountability, Motivation, and Processes needs to be much more intentional.

Tips to "RAMP Up" Your Virtual Team Performance

Relationships

One of the primary challenges faced by virtual teams is the lack of direct, face-to-face contact. Once team members settle into their habits and routines, it is easy to ignore the little things that

help build and reinforce the relationships necessary for sustaining a productive virtual team. High-performing teams compensate for the lack of human contact by identifying and focusing on people issues that exist on the team to foster team spirit, trust, and productivity.

David Kenny, CEO of Nielsen, shared that he builds relationships by getting people together for informal discussion. "We get the top 40 leaders together every Friday at noon. It's not structured and there is no set agenda. We go around, whether it's three minutes or a half hour, and I have one of my colleagues run it for me. This replaces what you learn at the coffee machine; now the whole world is around the coffee machine."

Gary Matthews, as CEO at a Houston-based electrical contracting and infrastructure firm during 2020, had a straightforward way to build relationships: He made a list of the top 75 leaders in the company and scheduled one-on-one video updates monthly. There was no business agenda; he asked about their families and tried to get a sense of their life outside of work. After a few monthly conversations, something unexpected happened. Despite the lack of a formal agenda, after a period of initial chitchat, team members began bringing up business issues. Ideas bubbled up. The sessions worked so well that Gary urged managers across the company to begin using the technique for their teams too.

Annie Adams, the chief transformation officer of Norfolk Southern, recalls how her company focused on constant contact – frequent communication centered not only on achieving business objectives but also on fostering personal connections and supporting employees. "We encouraged managers to proactively check on employees' mental and emotional health. We had a real focus on addressing anxiety," she says. "Managers needed to connect with people every day. We said, 'Don't let a day go by – try to maintain that level of connectedness. Make sure people don't get lost in the shuffle."

Although there's no shortage of technology that allows geographically distributed team members to interact and collaborate, the barriers of distance and time differences often make it hard to create a sense of community and trust. Fortunately, that same technology offers a variety of tools virtual leaders can use to help team members build relationships that allow them to work together more effectively. Here are a few creative virtual team-building activities companies are using today.

Conversation Channels

Most virtual teams utilize some form of software platform to facilitate communication and collaboration. Slack and Microsoft Teams are popular choices. These platforms accommodate multiple conversation threads and channels, most of which end up being dedicated to specific work topics. Setting up several nonwork conversation channels, however, is a good way for team members to engage in conversations that allow them to share interests or learn something about each other. While this might sound like a recipe for distraction, these channels serve the same function as general office conversations in a co-located work environment. Setting up a channel to discuss common topics like your favorite Netflix series, marathon training, childcare, or recipes gives virtual team members an opportunity to interact with one another in a different and ultimately constructive context.

Team-Building Software

Going a step beyond conversation channels, virtual teams can also install applications like Donut, which randomly pairs team members and schedules a video or in-person meeting between them. These meetings help team members to learn more about people with whom they might not regularly interact in the course of their work. Even if they know the other person already, a dedicated meeting encourages them to go beyond the basic pleasantries of typical office conversation and learn a bit more about their fellow team members, which helps to build trust.

Videos of Company Events

When working remotely, it's easy to lose sight of the big picture and become disengaged. Virtual team members spend so much time working on their own tasks that they don't have a good idea of how everything comes together to support the team's goals or the company's vision. Creating video segments that document company activities or provide a tangible example of how the team's work is making an impact can be motivating. If the video involves people who work on the team, they can be even more effective because it reinforces the sense that the team is collectively working toward something that's making a difference.

Quizzes

Quizzes are especially valuable as virtual team-building ice-breakers. Competitive quizzes can take a variety of forms and can be played in teams, but even simple quizzes that reveal people's interests and personality can contribute to entertaining conversations and provide insightful information. For instance, a quiz about which historical figure someone would choose to have dinner with, what items they would bring to a desert island, or what music they would pick for a long road trip can serve as an engaging conversation starter that encourages team members to share something about themselves, which can provide the foundation for future relationships. Many leaders of large virtual regional meetings send quizzes beforehand and use the data as part of the meeting introduction to get the group engaged.

Virtual Photo Competitions and Submissions

Thanks to smartphones, nearly everyone has a high-quality digital camera at their disposal. Photo competitions can give people an opportunity to use their creative side or share moments that are important to them. Halloween 2020 proved an especially creative time for people to share pictures of themselves and family members in distinctly COVID-19-inspired costumes and settings. Team members can even be encouraged to work together for some competitions, which can help promote collaboration in a team environment. Of course, not everything has to be a competition. Simply setting up a photo-sharing channel in Slack or Teams to allow people to post recent or memorable photos can help to build a sense of community within a team.

Coffee Meetings, Team Challenges, or Pizza Parties via Video

While it may be the most predictable entry on the list, scheduling time for a group to meet over coffee, whether to work or to discuss interests outside of work, is still one of the most effective ways for virtual team members to build stronger relationships with one another. This is especially useful if several people are in the same city or geographic area because it gives them an opportunity to meet and interact face to face. Even for geographically distributed teams, however, a virtual coffee meetup facilitated over video conferencing can be just as effective at overcoming virtual team-building challenges. Many virtual teams we work with use technology to have "coffee chats" to replicate what teams would do if they were in person. Other teams have virtual dinners where they highlight specific foods that are unique to different cultures to help team members learn about one another. Some companies offer cooking classes via Zoom or different workshops to build connectivity.

Digital "Bonfires"/All Company Meetings

A novel approach to virtual team building, a digital bonfire gathering is a regular meeting that involves not just a specific team, but the entire company. The online event features several message board topics that allow employees to engage with their own teams and people from other teams, which allows for relationships to form across functions. Guest speakers are often invited, and people can hold group video discussions or break off into smaller chats. Discovery, Inc.'s David Zaslav did just that to build community across the company during the many months of remote work. He hosted all-company global virtual meetings with a mixed agenda of an update about what was going on and then 30 minutes for guest speakers. These ranged from Discovery, Inc.'s own on-air personalities to inspiring external speakers sharing their expertise, including former Goldman Sachs CEO Lloyd Blankfein speaking about the '08 financial crisis, Hall of Fame tennis players Chris Evert and Boris Becker (who are commentators on Discovery, Inc.'s Eurosport network) speaking about how to compete under stress and anxiety, Zoom CEO Eric Yuan talking about technology and innovation, Congressman Hakeem Jeffries and film producer

Will Packer addressing systemic racial injustice, and Madeleine Albright sharing views on global geopolitics. While these interactive programs require coordination and effort, they can be tremendously helpful in building a strong organizational culture for a company that relies on a largely virtual workforce. Virtual team-building activities can help them to break the ice and get to know their fellow team members, which then paves the way toward building strong relationships based upon trust and respect.

Accountability

It happens to the best of teams. Things start out with a bang, with a virtual team getting a handle on the unique dynamics of working remotely and understanding how to perform at a high level. But like any other team, virtual teams often reach a point where they simply aren't making any gains in productivity. This is often known as the plateau effect. While performance may not be slipping (yet), a team that plateaus is in danger of becoming complacent and could easily begin to suffer from a lack of accountability and engagement. Successful virtual leaders find ways to overcome the plateau and get their team members reinspired. When it comes to virtual teams, there are a few simple strategies they can implement right away.

It is easy for team members to fall into predictable routines. This may make it easy for even outstanding employees to fade into the background and be taken for granted, especially in a virtual context where team members do not see each other very often. In some cases, their virtual team responsibilities may be in addition to their regular role, making them more likely to become distracted over time. Without feedback to acknowledge their performance, they may begin to feel as if their work isn't valued. Providing that feedback prevents them from feeling like they're undervalued. If they're doing things well, positive feedback can encourage them to keep producing.

By the time team members hit performance plateaus, it's generally safe to assume that they know what they're doing. This also means they might have some ideas on how things could be done better or how shaking up the status quo could improve results. Gathering feedback about team performance and processes also helps team members to think about how their role within the team could be developed, and what they could do to help accomplish goals more effectively.

It's also important that teams focus on a few critical metrics that are mutually supportive rather than numerous metrics that can lead to incompatible demands. Not only will this ensure individuals are motivated for team success, it will also encourage them to use team participation as a growth and development mechanism to improve their skills.

Tips to enhance accountability include:

- Ensure you understand each team members' role related to team decisions and activities.
- Have regular calls or check-in meetings to review progress on team goals or deliverables.
- Keep your promises and commitments. As soon as you realize that you cannot meet a commitment, let team members know and solicit their advice to get things done.
- Be willing to ask for help. Acknowledging that you may not be able to or have the time to carry out a particular responsibility but not discussing it with team members could delay progress and cause conflict amongst the team.
- Establish processes to periodically monitor team performance to determine whether the team is functioning effectively.

Motivation

When it comes to virtual teams, creating professional development plans and providing training to employees who want to build skills for the future helps them stay focused, delivering results and performing at a high level. By encouraging team members to improve and learn new skills, development programs (whether training, coaching, or job assignments), provide the tools for them to become more effective and confident. Promoting continuous learning has the added benefit of providing on-the-job experiences, keeping skills sharp, and helping people adapt to new situations more easily.

In companies, the shift to remote work has increased access to development opportunities. Kristin Yetto, chief people officer at eBay, said the old model of a "sage on the stage" who simply lectures via video has been replaced by more dynamic and interactive online development courses. When eBay shifted its diversity and inclusion training online during the pandemic, her team was able to quickly launch 20 classes in seven different languages, and even in their global company, they achieved over 90% participation – a dramatically lower no-show rate than they might have seen for in-person classes.

It is important for leaders to create a team culture that provides support and empathy when faced with challenges. In some cases, this could mean recognizing that someone is overburdened with tasks and may need some help. In other situations, simply being able to discuss challenges with fellow team members can help generate solutions. Resilient and motivated teams understand that they succeed or fail on the strength of their collaborative efforts, which makes them much more likely to raise concerns. Consider partnering people up or forming virtual subteams or pods so that people can stay connected from a distance. In essence, it is critical to foster a virtual support system.

As another form of feedback, the way teams are recognized can have a major impact on motivation and performance. Consider using different techniques for recognition, both individually and as a team. We discuss motivation extensively in Chapter 5, but highly effective virtual team leaders use a variety of techniques to recognize and motivate their employees. Perhaps the biggest component of motivation is infusing a sense of purpose.

If team members are simply going through the motions every day, they do not have any incentive to overcome challenges. Laying out a set of objectives for teams to accomplish is not the same as providing them with a sense of purpose that communicates why those objectives are important. Successful, motivated virtual teams are deeply committed to their goals because the work resonates on a personal level. Providing virtual teams with a sense of purpose should start with leaders building relationships with team members and understanding what motivates them. This allows them to draw connections between each person's values and the organization's mission. In addition, team members need to understand how their individual efforts contribute to a greater whole. When they recognize and value these connections, they will be more accountable to one another and more committed to overcoming challenges.

For instance, it is easy for lab scientists working for a large biotech company to lose sight of why their research matters. The work they do may be highly specialized and go unnoticed by company leadership. In order to keep them engaged and inspired in the face of challenges, leaders need to remind them how their work impacts patients and improves or saves people's lives. If an employee's motives and values align more closely with the company's goals, they will be more resilient in the face of challenges because they know their work is important.

In essence, find opportunities to focus on the big picture and remind your virtual team that their work is important. Invite guest speakers to join virtual meetings and find other ways to recognize the importance of the team's work. One of our clients regularly invites external customers to meetings to share challenges as well as talk about how the team's work contributes to their business strategy.

Strategies to help motivate virtual team members include:

- Brand your team. Create a group identity by developing a team name, slogan, logo, or other insignia. Team branding can be a great way to establish strong group identification and build team pride. One high-performing team created customized Yeti mugs with the team's logo – a Jim Collins–inspired flywheel – and each of their names emblazoned on a place on the flywheel.

- Take time at the beginning or end of a team call to review team and individual successes and accomplishments.

- Get to know what motivates each member of the team (e.g., affiliation, accomplishment, independence, safety, power, etc.) and try to assign work that aligns with those factors.

- Treat people as you expect to be treated. Communicate openly, honestly, and often.

- Frequently recognize successes, and make them visible, especially when other team members have significant achievements. For example, spotlight team accomplishments in a company or department newsletter or email distribution.

- Provide interesting assignments that are outside the normal work routine (make sure these types of assignments are given to everyone on the team, not just given to the one or two people you like the best or trust the most).

- Reinforce the team's sense of purpose by periodically reminding team members how what they are doing relates to the big picture.

- Involve team members in decisions that affect them by asking for their input and soliciting their feedback.

Process

Some companies and leaders assume that if they have the right technology their virtual teams will succeed on their own. As a result, they neglect other structural factors necessary for virtual teamwork. Technology is, of course, only a tool. While it's essential for virtual teams, our research shows that it's a prerequisite rather than a differentiator. Technological advancements will certainly continue to impact how people collaborate and work together from a distance, but best-in-class virtual leaders leverage technology and pay extra attention to the various processes that support remote teaming.

While some virtual team leaders communicate goals up front, they may neglect to update them as priorities shift. A common complaint from team members is that they aren't properly informed about changes in priorities and goals. One person we interviewed stated, "Our leader does not make sure that we know about changes to initiatives that affect our work, which is very frustrating. We often waste time and resources because we were not aware of a change." Another team member indicated, "My team leader does a better job updating team members who were in the same geographic location as he is, but he neglects to communicate key changes to team members in other locations." Unfortunately, ineffective communication and a lack of goal clarity can become more prevalent in a virtual setting.

The following tips will help establish clear process and goals for your virtual team:

- If the virtual team is too big, consider using subteams to ensure people have clear roles and contribute toward goals.

- Set expectations for communication and decision-making and reevaluate over time. For example, develop operating guidelines or rules of engagement to help structure team communication and coordination.

- To clarify who is held accountable for what, identify team members' roles and responsibilities. Revisit these roles and responsibilities regularly to determine if they need to be revised as goals and priorities evolve.

- Ensure the team has adequate resources to successfully accomplish its goals.

- Match technology to the task to ensure people are using technology well.

- Set up a process to assess whether the team is communicating and collaborating effectively and what it can do differently to be even more effective in these areas.

- Periodically collect feedback from stakeholders to assess the team's level of performance and identify barriers to high performance, as well as steps that can be taken.

In some cases, virtual teams are ineffective because their leaders and team members don't know how to overcome the challenges associated with working virtually. In these situations, as we've discussed in this chapter, the RAMP model provides specific guidelines and actions for ramping up team performance in four areas related to team success: *relationships*, *accountability*, *motivation*, and *process*.

The Bottom Line

- Effective virtual leaders recognize the importance of building relationships. They use technology (such as conversation channels and video), and virtual events (such as virtual coffees) to foster connectivity.

- Virtual leaders must be proactive about accountability and motivation. Checking in without a set agenda, following through on commitments, and coaching the team fosters accountability, empowerment, and motivation.

- Process is even important when working virtually. Set clear expectations about how the team will communicate, ensure that the team is informed about shifting priorities, and seek feedback from stakeholders about team performance over time.

5

Out of Sight, Not Out of Mind: How to Inspire and Motivate from Afar

M anaging a team of people who work remotely may seem easy, but many leaders are surprised to learn how challenging it can be. Virtual leaders need to make more of an effort in almost every sense. They need to be more proactive about building trust (as we discussed in Chapter 2), managing accountability and performance (as we've discussed in several chapters), and, perhaps most importantly, keeping employees motivated.

Why is it so challenging to motivate people from a distance? Here are a few critical reasons:

- Lack of visual cues can cause misunderstandings, making effective delegation more difficult.
- Team members may not directly interact with clients or co-workers and may not see a clear link between their work and business outcomes.
- The tendency to focus on task rather than relationship when working virtually makes it less likely virtual leaders will take the time to listen and demonstrate an interest in people.
- Infrequent interaction makes it difficult to build relationships with team members and understand their values and aspirations.
- Distance and the reliance on technology make it difficult to create a sense of purpose.
- Leaders may struggle finding ways to intellectually stimulate the team via virtual communication channels, which are more complex and cognitively taxing than face-to-face communication.

Inspirational leadership involves aligning values with initiatives to create enthusiasm and a passion to act. Leaders who do this successfully light a fire within others, resulting in higher performance and more sustained effort. Inspired teams are more likely to meet goals and demonstrate high levels of engagement with their work. This leads to lower instances of absenteeism, improved overall quality of work, and increased productivity. Despite the many benefits of inspirational leadership, some leaders struggle to inspire their teams. How can leaders inspire and engage those around them despite being geographically dispersed?

A *Harvard Business Review* article[1] published in April 2020 by Lindsay McGregor and Neel Doshi found that leaders do three key things to motivate people in a virtual setting. First, they create a fun environment while at work. Next, they create a sense of purpose where people can have visibility into their impact on clients or other stakeholders. And finally, they create the conditions for employees to get opportunities for growth and learning.

Although some research shows remote employees tend to be happier and more productive compared to their peers with less workplace flexibility, it can be more difficult for them to stay motivated if they don't feel connected to the rest of their team. Therefore, leaders need to be more mindful and deliberate to ensure that they are focusing on these motivators with their remote employees. Here are four ways leaders can leverage the concepts of play, purpose, and potential to keep remote employees engaged and motivated to reach their full potential.

Find Ways to Recognize and Reward Employees

Coaching and giving feedback (which we cover in Chapter 9) is important, but it is also vital to acknowledge employees' achievements. You can do this in both formal ways, such as official weekly shout-outs via email or social media, and in the moment as you notice employees going above and beyond. Recognition should always be specific and behavioral. General praise doesn't allow for people to understand what they did correctly and know to continue doing it.

Even if they're separated by hundreds or thousands of miles, high-functioning virtual teams are still committed to both individual and collective success. That can be easy to forget when they're isolated from one another and don't see the connections between the work they do and the outcome of the team's labor.

Taking time to celebrate both individual performance and other wins can remind team members that each person's contributions matter to the team's success.

Get to Understand the Values of Your Remote Team Members

Because inspiring team members requires that leaders make an appeal to others' emotions, values, or beliefs, becoming an inspirational leader *requires* an understanding of each. This means finding out what motivates them and makes them truly excited for the time ahead. Knowing what team members enjoy and value about their work helps leaders better understand how to best motivate them; it also helps to know how their job fits in with other aspects of their life. Employees with spouses and children, for instance, will have a different conception of work-life balance than those without. Managing a diverse team with fairness and equity requires leaders to understand and respect those expectations.

Having information about an employee's interests outside of work can be helpful for knowing how to inspire them. What do an employee's hobbies say about their values? Does the employee participate in a volunteer organization? Are they signed up to do a virtual marathon? Are they writing a screenplay on the side? Knowing about and showing interest in an employee's hobbies demonstrates care, which can have an inspirational effect in and of itself.

The good news is that the rapid shift to a virtual setting has given leaders permission to be even more curious and authentic when interacting remotely. Many of us get to learn more about our colleagues when children are running into the room during Zoom meetings, pets are making an appearance on camera, and we have been able to get a view of people outside of work. And just as we mentioned in remote interviewing, a technique to build understanding of your virtual team members is to take advantage of the unique possibilities afforded by the technology medium. Ask your colleague to show you the pictures on the bookshelf or to give you a tour of the kitchen and hear the stories behind the items.

Help the Team Find Its "Why?" and Then Focus on the "How"

Simon Sinek, a well-known motivational speaker and author of *New York Times* best-selling books, such as *Leaders Eat Last: Why Some Teams Pull Together and Others Don't*, talks at length about answering the question of "why" in his TED talks about inspiring others to action:[2]

> Every single person, every single organization on the planet knows what they do, 100 percent. . . . But very, very few people or organizations know why they do what they do. And by "why" I don't mean "to make a profit." That's a result. It's always a result. By "why," I mean: What's your purpose? What's your cause? What's your belief? Why does your organization exist? Why do you get out of bed in the morning? And why should anyone care? As a result, the way we think, we act, the way we communicate is from the outside in, it's obvious. We go from the clearest thing to the fuzziest thing. But the inspired leaders and the inspired organizations – regardless of their size, regardless of their industry – all think, act and communicate from the inside out.

One aspect that separates truly inspirational leaders from their peers is the ability to understand and explain the "why" of their organization to others. Leaders start with answering "why" because, once their team understands that, they know they aren't just driving profits so others can make money; they're making a difference in people's lives, in their industry, community, or world at large.

Create a Sense of Purpose and then Focus on the "How"

Answering the "why" of the organization is one way to inspire others. However, that isn't always enough. Leaders must also find ways to create a sense of purpose for their team. This begins with a bit of self-reflection. Have the organization's goals been clearly and explicitly communicated to the team? Do employees understand how they make a difference in the big picture? Do they have a sense of pride and ownership in what they're doing?

Brian Goldner, chairman and CEO of play and entertainment company Hasbro, described the way they have focused on linking purpose to the "how." "We've always been a purpose-led company – Hasbro's mission is to create the world's best play experiences, and our purpose is to make the world a better place for all children and all families.

The best play experiences stand apart from anyone else's and deliver joy, creativity, and connection around the world and across generations. But we've changed the way we communicate," he said. "We've gone beyond our visionary, strategic statements to find ways in which people can understand how they literally impact the business." Brian explained that in managing through 2020, the company set four priorities to continue to operate and deliver on its mission: supply, demand, liquidity, and community. And he and all the company's managers have worked with teams and individuals to concretely develop actions to support one of the four priorities: "How do we get new modalities of production with creative and get our TV and film projects done (supply)? How can we innovate and create new play experiences for families undergoing lockdown and what future storytelling and IP projects are we creating and what new marketing content are we developing to drive e-commerce (demand)? On liquidity, our finance teams are ensuring that our investors, banks, suppliers, and accounts receivable are managed to ensure we have adequate cash and liquidity to run our business. And on community, HR and management teams have been engaged with every individual in our company to understand if they have kids at home or an elderly parent, what their ability to work at home is, and how can we support them. With those component parts, everyone at a distance can ask themselves how they are contributing to one of those four priorities."

Brian shared how his early life experience before he went into business informed his management approach. "I learned early on from leading trips in the great outdoors that you need guideposts. You give expedition members training, maps, and tools and each day before the outing you agree on the objective (where to arrive and when). Then you let people take responsibility and get on with it. It's the same way with leading at a distance. We need to have a shared understanding of where we're going and then help people see how what they are doing is contributing and fitting in."

An inspirational leader shows them how their work makes a difference, both to their team and the company as a whole.

Empowering employees strengthens their connection to the organization and helps them align their goals with the rest of their team. Leaders can promote empowerment by providing realistic challenges to motivate people as well as champion collaboration to bolster a sense of community. When employees feel like they have the tools for success and understand what they're working to achieve together, they are more productive and engaged.

In our discussion with Tony Thelan from John Deere Financial, he emphasized the importance of empowerment when working virtually. "We empowered people by allowing them to make decisions faster in a virtual environment, which enhanced performance and engagement."

Here is a quick self-assessment to see how you are doing in the area of creating a sense of purpose with your virtual team and employees:

Directions: In order to determine how you create meaning and purpose for your team, rate yourself on the sense of purpose items using the following scale:

5 = I do a great job of this.

3 = I do an OK job of this.

1 = I really don't do this at all.

1. Organization

___ Help my virtual team have an explicitly clear understanding of our organizational purpose – as a company or for our specific group (more than making money)

___ Communicate a very clear vision of where we need to go in the future; something to strive for – as a company or for our specific group

____ Communicate, live by, and reinforce a distinct set of values – as a company or for our specific group

2. Relationship to the Organization

____ Help each of my people feel like they make a difference

____ Encourage continuous improvement and innovation

____ Keep my people connected to the "big picture" regularly

3. Self

____ Create a workplace in which people can pursue their personal values

____ Give people challenges that are motivating and realistic

____ Create, support, and reinforce associate learning and development

____ Ensure people have what they need to achieve their goals

4. Relationship to Others

____ Build a sense of community, despite being virtual

____ Champion collaboration, helping others, and cooperation

____ Keep a constant focus on the customer

____ Seek to involve others to create a sense of ownership

Use the results of this quick self-assessment to help create an action plan for building a sense of purpose with your virtual team. For example, perhaps bring in guest speakers who can recognize or show appreciation for the team's efforts. Have virtual lunch-and-learns or coffee chats that focus on how the team's efforts impact the broader organization.

Become a Storyteller

One of the key traits of inspirational leaders noted by Jack Zenger and Joseph Folkman in their *Harvard Business Review* article[3] is that "inspirational leaders are more adept at making emotional connections with their subordinates." Part of being able to make an emotional connection is being an effective storyteller, which means being able to take ideas and put them into a context that allows the listener to understand them.

One notable example shared with us about telling stories to engage employees comes from Adaire Fox-Martin, executive board member of Customer Success at global software company SAP. "I started writing a weekly note to the entire team (40,000 people around the world). I called it 'The week that was.' I include some things that happened professionally and other things personally. I did 20 of them for 20 weeks. The response has been incredible with people sharing back experiences in their lives and business. It maintained and deepened a sense of global community."

A similar approach has been used with great effect by Betsy Bradley, president of Vassar College. Betsy sends a weekly "Sunday Email" to the entire Vassar community of students, parents, and many alumni (of which Jim is one!) that has become a must-read. It's an informal and engaging multimedia report of happenings on campus told with colorful stories, photos, and videos. Here's an example of the tone and content from the end of 2020:

Dear all,

WE MADE IT! After the whole semester we had about 45 positive COVID-19 tests among students, after 16,168 tests . . . a rate of 0.002 positives and 99.8% negative. All cases were asymptomatic, and we had no on-campus spread. CONGRATULATIONS, VASSAR! Happy Winter Break! I hope you all are going to have some down time next week and can relax before the final weeks of the semester. For many of you, this is a major transition to remote learning and hopefully you can stay healthy and safe wherever you are.

One Inc.com article[4] highlights a few effective strategies for using storytelling in a business setting – such as establishing time, place, people, events, surprise, relevance, and emotion in a small story. Why a small story? Because, as the article notes, small stories are "the anecdotes concerning real-life experiences that people tell every day in conversations." These are the kind of stories people hear and tell one another all the time, so they're easy to understand for most employees.

In the article, author Shawn Callahan states, "Told consistently over time, small stories will help employees understand the concrete actions needed to get a job done, how to bring a value to life, and how to implement a strategy." By using small stories effectively, leaders can communicate their vision to their employees in a way that the employee can understand and even internalize. This, in turn, helps inspire the employee to help the leader fulfill their vision.

Effective leaders utilize a variety of strategies to get the most out of their teams, but they share a foundation of active communication and engagement. Getting to know team members as individuals and showing them how they contribute to the organization's success can instill their work with a strong sense of purpose. By using easy-to-understand stories to communicate the company's vision, leaders also build the trust that helps their teams achieve their goals. Here are a few practical tips to help you become even more effective at storytelling from a distance:

- Be honest and authentic – connect with people to check in even with no agenda.

- Your story should reflect your values – try to infuse your values into meetings or other forums.

- Show and share emotions even when it means exposing anxieties, fears, and shortcomings.

- Understand what your audience knows, cares about, and wants to hear about – get feedback on your virtual meetings and find ways to build in the team's feedback to convey that you are listening.

- Interact with listeners, make the "I" of the story "we;" put them in the center of the story and invite them to join you or your quest.

- Tailor the story to the situation; never tell the story the same way twice.

- Prepare obsessively but be ready to drop the script and improvise.

- Offer a value proposition that is worthy of the audience.

- Express your values and call for others to adopt.

The Bottom Line

- Motivating people at a distance is challenging because of the lack of in-person contact, which can make it harder to understand what motivates people and to convey the team's sense of purpose.

- Leaders can enhance a team's sense of purpose by focusing on the "why" of their work. Focus not on the day-to-day goals, but on the larger impact of the virtual team's work – on the company and its customers, on the industry, or on society. Invite guest speakers, send videos, and find creative ways to reinforce the "why" and only then focus on the "how."

- One technique for virtual motivation is storytelling. A good story emphasizes the time, place, and people; describes the events that took place; and does so in a way that creates a sense of surprise. Because telling a story virtually requires slightly more performance than telling one in person, it can be useful to rehearse a story – but when telling it, favor authenticity over a scripted feel.

Notes

1 Lindsay McGregor and Neel Doshi, "How to Keep Your Team Motivated, Remotely," *Harvard Business Review*, April 9, 2020, https://hbr.org/2020/04/how-to-keep-your-team-motivated-remotely.

2 Simon Sinek, "How great leaders inspire action," TEDx, Puget Sound, September 2009, www.ted.com/talks/simon_sinek_how_great_leaders_inspire_action/transcript?language=en.

3 Jack Zenger and Joseph Folkman, "What Inspiring Leaders Do," *Harvard Business Review*, June 20, 2013, https://hbr.org/2013/06/what-inspiring-leaders-do.

4 Alison Davis, "The Surprising Way to Be More Effective at Storytelling," *Inc.*, February 6, 2018, www.inc.com/alison-davis/the-surprising-way-to-be-more-effective-at-storytelling.html.

6

"You're on Mute": The Ultimate Guide for Hosting Virtual Meetings

Many companies were surprised by how productive employees could be when everyone was suddenly forced to work remotely during the pandemic. There are some obvious reasons for that, such as the elimination of commutes. But there's one overlooked factor as to why remote work can be so productive. When run well, virtual meetings can be startlingly efficient.

That's one of the lessons David Calhoun, CEO of Boeing, shared he drew from his early months as a full-time remote leader. Boeing is a global company with a headquarters in Chicago, large manufacturing facilities in Washington State and South Carolina, key stakeholders in Washington, D.C., and important customers all around the world. As CEO, Dave needs to meet with people in all these places, and even for someone with access to his own 737 aircraft, the logistics and travel time can be daunting.

"Video meetings are amazingly effective for the personal efficiency of a CEO," he said. "You can waste half a day on logistics going to and from [in-person] meetings, but now you can call any meeting and get it done. I can reach more people by far than before and more quickly. I can do six or eight substantive meetings in a day, when before I would have had to travel for each one." And it's not just about reducing travel time. When everyone worked in offices, simply scheduling a meeting with an internal Boeing team could take days because of the challenge of getting everyone to be in the same place at the same time. With everyone working from home, Dave calls an internal meeting on an hour or two of notice, knowing that people will often be able to rearrange their schedules to be in front of their camera if he needs them. "I can call a meeting in a short cycle, dial everyone in, and get it done," he told us.

Dave doesn't expect his reliance on video for every meeting to last forever. "I'll go back to traveling when all is safe, but not the same way," he said. "I will do as much or more customer travel, because that's still the most important way to build relationships. But most travel when leading big companies is visiting your own teams. I won't be doing that nearly as much." Dave said that when people do a good job of adapting a meeting to the constraints of video, "the digital tools do a better job for meetings than being there in person."

Part of that last sentence bears repeating: Video meetings work well *when people do a good job of adapting to the medium.* Research suggests too few people are making this shift. Only 62% of people are somewhat satisfied with the virtual meetings they attend, and 73% report "getting everyone engaged" and "multi-tasking" are always or often challenging.[1] With users of Microsoft Teams conducting 2.7 billion minutes of online meetings during a single day in 2020,[2] the math is not encouraging. There are far too many people spending too much time in meetings that aren't being run well.

Inefficient meetings are not just roadblocks to productivity. They can also kill motivation and engagement, sapping employees of their commitment to their work – leaving them thinking, "Why do I need to even be here?" Because these meetings are often the primary means of communication and collaboration for virtual teams, making them effective and engaging is crucial – but because the shift to video meetings was so sudden, very few leaders were trained on how to lead meetings effectively in this medium.

In this chapter, we'll explain why virtual meetings need to be organized and run differently than physical meetings – and how to do it right.

Before the Meeting

Confirm That a Meeting Is Really Necessary

Some meetings shouldn't happen in the first place. Research from Clarizen and Harris Interactive[3] indicates that 59% of leaders report spending more time preparing for a status meeting than time on the meeting itself. Further, 60% of respondents indicated that they multitask during status update meetings – a sure sign they aren't fully engaged. Instead of running status meetings out of habit, consider whether you really need a meeting to achieve your objectives. Justin Hale and Joseph Grenny of the training firm VitalSmarts recommend only having a virtual meeting to accomplish one of the four objectives: to solve problems, to make decisions, to gain buy-in and support, or to build relationships.[4] If your meeting isn't aimed at achieving one of these four goals, there's a good chance you shouldn't be scheduling it.

Jeff Teper, Microsoft corporate vice president and leader of the Teams video communications platform, shared that he urges leaders to analyze the "rhythm of the business" and *not* to let the use of the virtual meeting tools be organic. The trap is that because it is so simple to schedule meetings, make video calls, or send chats, you can do these without consideration for the impact on others. Jeff advises leaders to look at their workflows, the information that needs to be communicated, the decisions that need to be made, and the style of key decision makers and use all of that to design an optimal process. Of course, you want to use the tools available, but you and your teams will benefit by applying them with a light touch and the flexibility to adapt the medium to the objective.

There are cases when emails or an audio-only meeting can be a better format than a video meeting. Some experts classify communication media and tools by their "richness." This includes factors such as the capacity for feedback, visual cues, and sense of personal connection. If face-to-face meetings are the "richest" form of communication, video would be second, followed by telephone, and email/text messaging would be last.

In some situations, emails – though the least "rich" form of communication – can be more valuable than arranging a conference call or video meeting. Unlike the spoken word, email is easily shared, can be read several times to aid comprehension, and can be referred to long after it's sent. When a leader's sole objective is to share information, email may be a good choice. However, when you're seeking to engage the hearts and minds of others, to have genuine dialogue, coach someone, or deal with conflict, then video meetings are infinitely superior to email. By matching your communication methods to the goal you have in mind, you will save time, and in some cases eliminate the need for a meeting altogether.

Build an Effective Meeting Agenda

Every meeting – in person or not – should have an agenda. But agendas are especially important for v-meetings, because when people are participating remotely, it's especially easy for people to zone out. We hear about regularly scheduled virtual meetings, or v-meetings, that are conducted without agendas, but they take place because they are on the calendar. Just as with in-person meetings, poorly run virtual meetings not only waste time, but they jeopardize the team's ability to meet its deadlines. This is especially true when people are on multiple virtual teams that each have routine meetings – these employees can quickly lose control of their schedules and have little time for heads-down work. Even for small virtual meetings with close colleagues, it's dramatic how much more effective they will be if you distribute a suggested agenda of a few bullet points to keep everyone on track.

Determine who needs to attend and invite participants, giving them as much advance notice as possible. Next, ensure that your meeting agenda is engaging so that people are more apt to participate. Instead of giving every agenda item equal time, spend more time on priority issues. If there is relevant background information, or someone will be presenting slides, send them in advance. Meetings that focus on discussion, rather than presenting information, are not only more enjoyable, they're also typically a better use of people's precious time. When building the agenda, recognize that many people struggle to remain engaged in long virtual meetings. For example, many companies are accustomed to conducting semi-annual, in-person "offsite" meetings that may last all day. Trying to replicate this on video screens is a mistake. Virtual meetings should be short and focused – and if that requires holding three one-hour meetings instead of a single three-hour meeting, that's the right choice.

Overcoming Time Zone Barriers When Scheduling V-meetings

One of the biggest difficulties is finding a meeting time that works well for all team members, especially for global teams whose members may span multiple time zones. Team members often complain of having to work longer hours – working at 10:00 p.m. or even having to get up at 3:00 a.m. – to accommodate their virtual teams. Effective virtual leaders rotate meeting times so that the same team members do not always get stuck working at undesirable hours. And if the purpose of the meeting is just information sharing, the most effective virtual teams find alternative ways to share the information – ranging from email to recording a video presentation that can be viewed later – without requiring people to get on a live call at an inconvenient hour. Recognizing this, Lori Goler, VP of People at Facebook, shared that the social media juggernaut made it a priority to adapt from all-live meetings to sharing information and tasks asynchronously.

Running the Meeting

The Facilitator's Role

The virtual meeting facilitator plays a crucial role in making v-meetings a worthwhile experience. He or she guides the process, encourages suggestions, keeps the team on track, creates a positive climate, and anticipates pitfalls. Great facilitators are prepared to interrupt discussions when necessary to realign the team with the meeting's goal, refocus it on the agenda, and help it improve its productivity.

Naturally, active participation is very important during virtual meetings. But how can a facilitator make sure everyone is participating when the meeting is being held over the phone or via a videoconference? The key is to listen closely and be patient with the team's progress.

In high-performing virtual teams, team members often take on a facilitation role as needed, depending on the meeting objectives. Everyone takes responsibility for keeping the group on track, ensuring that time is well-managed, and ensuring that meeting objectives are being met.

To reinforce the shared nature of the meeting, arrange for different people to lead parts of the session. If appropriate, you can even ask team members to rotate the facilitator role itself. Having different people lead different parts of the virtual meeting can improve participation. Additionally, it can be an effective way to keep team members from checking out during meetings.

Maintain High Levels of Engagement

Part of keeping people engaged depends on relationships: the more that people trust each other, the more engaged they tend to be. Conduct meetings with an eye not only to transacting business, but to deepening relationships. As people sign on, greet them and make small talk.

Mary Dillon, the CEO of Ulta Beauty, said one of the things she misses the most is the fun, informal banter she loves to have with her team and associates, so she has been making time for those moments. Whether it is putting up fun balloon backgrounds to celebrate good news, asking about remote learning impacts for parents, or pulling out her "You're on Mute" sign at least once a meeting, she keeps the personal connection while also leading business discussions.

To ensure interaction, make sure the people on the call need to be there and know what is expected from them in terms of participation. Vary the way you solicit feedback, such as using polls or Yes/No buttons. When meetings are small and participants are in quiet locations, encourage people to lay off the Mute button to allow more spontaneous interaction. Gerri Martin-Flickinger, CTO of Starbucks, shared with us that she uses Wordles, a word cloud generator, and Kahoot, an interactive meeting platform, in virtual meetings to foster dialogue and engage people.

Ensuring the right meeting breaks may seem like a small thing, but for everyone who has become antsy toward the top of the hour with no break in sight, this is a big deal. The meeting leader should signal when the meeting breaks will occur and stick to the schedule as promised. It's been said that sitting is the new smoking. So, for all remote workers who don't have stand-up desks, encourage participants to stand up periodically during the meeting. And when it's time for the break, give enough break time to allow colleagues to go outside for fresh air, to stretch, get a few steps in, or go to the kitchen to get a beverage. Gerri encourages time between meetings to provide leaders with time for context switching, which allows people time to go for a quick walk or take a break to mentally prepare for the next virtual meeting.

Stay on Track

How do top virtual leaders keep everyone on track during the meeting? They use process intervention techniques when necessary to keep the team focused. An example of this is interrupting a discussion to refocus the participants and/or rebalance group interactions. Although process intervention can be challenging in a virtual setting due to more limited visual cues (other than hand waving), it becomes critical to success.

One important technique is observation – pay close attention to the flow of the discussion. Are the comments and issues being raised aligned with the stated agenda? Also, attend to team members' interactions by focusing on behaviors. Keep in mind that you won't have as much of an ability to discern meeting participants' body language or other visual cues as fully as in person. Therefore, it is important to keep up with the level of participation of individual members and to listen carefully to their tone and words. Paraphrasing is an easy way to confirm your understanding of a team member's comments before you intervene. And as a virtual meeting leader, pay attention to the chat feature that has become a standard part of meeting interactions. Often, especially in large group meetings, the chat dialogue can be just as rich a source of information as the comments that are shared aloud.

Know Your Audience and Plan Accordingly

It is important to distinguish between meetings in which everyone is participating virtually by video, and those in which some portion of participants are physically together (e.g., in a conference room). When possible, try to avoid mixing the two since it is difficult to meet the needs of both audiences when they are in the same meeting. For example, a single remote attendee will have greater difficulty hearing low-volume discussions and reading nonverbal cues. In some cases, this can lead to frustration or feelings of isolation. When you have a combined audience, facilitators need to describe what is happening locally among the in-person participants to keep people engaged. If possible, however, make it a rule that if anyone is alone during a virtual meeting, then perhaps everyone is alone – even if that means asking a group of people to leave the conference room and participate by video from their own desks.

Cross-Cultural Tips

Video meetings can be particularly challenging when participants come from different regions and speak different native languages. To try to overcome them, demonstrate that you welcome these differences. Show a genuine interest in the traditions, geographies, and even politics of team members' locations. Be aware of other countries' holidays, national sports obsessions, and cultural festivals. During virtual lunches or coffee breaks, share the food of a particular country.

When some participants are not native speakers of the language being used in a meeting, recognize that. Allow more time on the agenda to be sure people understand. Avoid jargon, acronyms, and metaphors that don't translate across cultures or languages. Use paraphrasing and active listening to avoid misunderstanding. Consider using tools such as polls or chat boxes that allow people to share opinions without having to speak audibly.

Recognize that different cultures have different expectations of etiquette in meetings. Although North and South Americans are quick to use first names, some Asian or traditional European cultures prefer more formal address, so ask before shifting to a first-name basis. Understand norms around punctuality when it comes to meeting start times and to deadlines. Be prepared to be flexible when expectations on these issues are different, but work to clarify and agree on them.

The Five Types of Disruptors in Virtual Meetings and How to Handle Them

In a virtual setting, where a person can use the camera angle or video mute to hide, it's easy to develop bad meeting habits. People who fall into this trap can be grouped into one of five primary

archetypes. Learning to recognize and address them is key to running an effective virtual meeting.

The Multitasker

This person spends time in virtual meetings doing email or working on projects in the belief that it will be a more efficient use of their time. They're often distracted and they distract others. One global financial services CEO lamented that on a management committee video meeting, one of the senior executives, wearing attire suggesting he was heading out to the golf course after the meeting, was on the screen for several minutes speaking on his iPhone, clearly oblivious to how discourteous and distracting he was to others. To limit people from multitasking, ask participants to enable their webcams, require people to comment – even if it means cold-calling them for their views – and set expectations up front in terms of meeting ground rules (including that people won't multitask). As mentioned above, also schedule shorter meetings with focused agendas.

The Noise-Bringer

Sometimes, employees have little choice but to start a virtual meeting in a busy environment that has a lot of background noise. However, some seem to forget that the noise around them can be disruptive. To counter people who bring too much back-ground noise with them, ask people to mute themselves except when they are speaking. If it's a large group, you can take con-trol as the meeting host and put everyone except the current speaker on mute.

The Disorganized and Late

In any team, there can be members who struggle to remain organized, coming late to meetings because they feel they are too busy, or perhaps they're absentminded. The late arrival of these members disrupts the flow of a meeting. Some effective counters for this disruptive virtual team members include ask-ing habitually late meeting members to log in a few minutes early and turning off the "doorbell" greeting that announces a new caller joining to prevent interruptions when late comers join.

The Interrupter

In meetings there are times when providing insight and input is valuable. However, the interrupter tends to talk over people and be disrespectful of their opinions, causing friction and dis-rupting the conversation. One tactic to counter the interrupter is to announce a queue for questions and comments (e.g., "Hold on, George, first we have Connie and then Jason and then we'll come to you."). Another is to give meeting feedback offline to make the interrupter aware of his impact on others, stressing that it limits effectiveness and destroys trust. You can coach the person, offering encouragement to perform a mental countdown before interjecting in a conversation – providing time to think about the comment he wants to offer.

The Checked Out

With these employees, the lights are on, but nobody's home. These participants are typically seen but not heard – failing to respond or show initiative. This checked-out, indifferent attitude prevents employees from getting the benefit out of the meeting or adding value to others. Some counters for these nonparticipants include ensuring that each attendee is responsible for at least one item on the agenda – giving them incentive to pay attention, sending recap emails following a meeting, and holding each participant responsible for their actions.

By being aware of these five kinds of disruptive people in virtual meetings and taking measures to reduce the problems they cause, you will vastly improve the effectiveness of your meetings.

A Few Important Caveats About Media Richness: Video Burnout

Although the richness of video meetings is one reason why remote work has become so much more effective than it was in the years before broadband, there are downsides. One of the most significant is what many of us who have worked relentlessly at a distance have experienced, "Zoom burnout." New research shows that people who spend too much time in video meetings suffer the not surprising condition of burnout and cognitive fatigue. While video is the closest to face-to-face interaction in

terms of visual cues and other elements of media richness, there are some very important differences that cause cognitive fatigue.

Microsoft's World Trend Index[5] reveals that brainwave patterns associated with stress and overwork are significantly higher when working virtually. In essence, remote work is more cognitively challenging. The study also found that brainwave markers associated with stress are also much higher in video meetings than nonmeeting work. In video meetings, people must work hard to continuously focus on the screen to identify information and remain engaged. Because we are focusing on a screen, we're seeing fewer nonverbal cues that would normally help us interpret interactions, which means that we must work harder to communicate. Perhaps most importantly, video calls can seem unnatural, with people staring at one another for prolonged periods of time. In a real meeting room, we look in different directions instead of always staring at the person who's talking. Gallery view, in which a group of people are on the screen together, can seem impersonal and further exacerbate these problems. And it's exceptionally difficult not to be conscious of how you appear in the corner of the display. It can also be exhausting. Delays and other technology issues make video discussions less natural as well. As a result, many technology companies are working to improve the video experience and combat some of these issues. Sheryl Sandberg, COO of Facebook, points to the brisk pace of video meetings as one cause of the burnout. "Things get more formal on Zoom, so it is important to have the informal banter at the beginning of the meeting," she said. "That can encourage interaction and help overcome video fatigue."

Here are a few tips to help combat video fatigue.

- Take regular breaks.
- Have video-free days or meeting-free days. Google[6] officially has no meeting days *and* weeks to encourage flexibility.

- Consider having 20-minute meetings (instead of 30 minutes) or 50-minute meetings (rather than 60 minutes) to allow people "transition time."

- Make video social events optional so that people do not feel obligated to attend after a long day of video calls. Some teams we work with only use video for some calls, or they only use it for portions of their calls to help offset these problems. One leader we spoke to said that she received very negative feedback using Zoom for lunch meetings. "Imagine staring at yourself eating a sandwich or salad while on video – it is not pleasant," she said. She's right.

- Take calls from outdoors, or from different indoor locations, to reduce some of the cognitive fatigue. There is evidence that "walking meetings" enhance creativity and reduce stress.

- Experiment with different technologies that help make us feel like we are "together" in meetings. For example, Microsoft released a Together mode to digitally project people into the same shared background, which makes it easier to pick up on visual cues. Microsoft believes that this mode allows people to engage with one another in a more spontaneous and natural way. Imagine being "in a meeting room" or a "coffee bar" instead of the traditional grid view used in most video technology. Jeff Teper, leader for Teams, said, "Humans are social beings who connect emotionally using body language and verbal cues to build feelings of trust, and part of what makes a team is a shared purpose and sense of trust. Together mode is rooted in human psychology and sociology."[7]

- Use the focus status in Teams, or block time in your calendar, to make room for breaks, creative activities, or just to disconnect in between meetings.

- Some researchers suggest sitting sideways to avoid staring at the camera for the entire video meeting. In video calls, it is unnatural to stare so intently at people without taking notes or doing other things, yet people are concerned that if they stop looking at the camera, that they will be perceived as not paying attention. When we are sitting around a conference table, it is natural for people to have sidebar discussions or take notes, so we need to be aware of this on video calls.

- Use direct eye contact when speaking. Lori Johnston, CHRO of Amgen, told us that after receiving this training tip from a former BBC on air presenter, she tapes a photo of her granddaughter to the top of her camera to look at during video conferences. The effect is that it makes her appear natural and happy during virtual meetings. This also overcomes a tendency to stare at the screen rather than at the camera when they speak, making them less connected with and less natural to their audience.

- Avoid multitasking during video chats, which makes our cognitive fatigue even worse.

- Use plain backgrounds when you appear on group video chats. This helps reduce some of the cognitive work associated with excess stimuli since we process visual cues such as different backgrounds in video calls.

- One company we interviewed provides coaching and training to leaders on how to come across as genuine, comfortable, and authentic when using video to communicate, which has had a tremendous response. One technique they suggest: move your hands and body, using nonverbal cues just as you would in a physical meeting, to try to seem more relaxed. Of course, it is important to avoid excessive movement that can be distracting.

Some of the techniques we describe in this chapter may not come instinctively. But in our research, one thing we've discovered is that when leaders begin practicing intentionally to become better at using virtual meeting technologies, the improvements come quickly and dramatically. "Now that everyone has a chance to speak, the meetings have become much more democratic, and we're making better decisions," said Hans Vestberg, chairman and CEO of Verizon.

That's the kind of improvement for which every leader should aim.

The Bottom Line

- Video meetings, when carefully managed, can work just as well as in-person meetings. When employees complain about "Zoom burnout," it is often a sign that meetings are not effective. Ensure a meeting is necessary, create a short agenda, and ensure interactivity to engage team members.
- During v-meetings, appoint a facilitator (who may or may not be the team leader), work to keep people engaged, vary the way you solicit feedback, and maintain a balance between working on tasks and building relationships.
- Recognize that virtual meetings are especially prone to disruption. Learn to recognize the five most common types of meeting disruptors and have a plan for addressing them.

Notes

1 Rick Lepsinger, "Practical Tips for Successful Virtual Leadership," HRDQ-U Webinars, accessed December 1, 2020,

www.hrdqu.com/leadership-style-assessment/practical-tips-successful-virtual-leadership/.

2 Jared Spataro, "Remote work trend report: meeting," Microsoft 365 (blog), April 9, 2020, www.microsoft.com/en-us/microsoft-365/blog/2020/04/09/remote-work-trend-report-meetings/.

3 Jen Howard, "Clarizen Survey says Employees in the U.S. Waste Up To 30 Percent of Work Week on Status Meetings," Clarizen, February 9, 2016, www.clarizen.com/press-release/clarizen-survey-says-employees-in-the-u-s-waste-up-to-30-percent-of-work-week-on-status-meetings/.

4 Justin Hale and Joseph Grenny, "How to Get People to Actually Participate in Virtual Meetings," *Harvard Business Review*, March 9, 2020, https://hbr.org/2020/03/how-to-get-people-to-actually-participate-in-virtual-meetings.

5 Jared Spataro, "The future of work—the good, the challenging & the unknown," Microsoft 365 (blog), July 8, 2020, www.microsoft.com/en-us/microsoft-365/blog/2020/07/08/future-work-good-challenging-unknown/.

6 Jason Aten, "Google's 3-Word Plan to Help Employees Avoid Burnout Is So Simple You Should Steal It," *Inc.*, November 17, 2020, www.inc.com/jason-aten/googles-3-word-plan-to-help-employees-avoid-burnout-is-so-simple-you-should-steal-it.html.

7 Susanna Ray, "Video fatigue and a late-night host with no audience inspire a new way to help people feel together, remotely," Microsoft Innovation Stories (blog), July 8, 2020, https://news.microsoft.com/innovation-stories/microsoft-teams-together-mode/.

7

Hiring Without a Handshake: Discovering Successful Virtual Leaders

It was almost midnight on a Sunday in March 2020. The COVID-19 pandemic was accelerating, and our firm faced a dilemma. For the prior two months, we'd been working with the board of directors of eBay on the search for a new CEO, and we were at a critical juncture. We'd led discussions with dozens of potential candidates, winnowed the list, and worked with the eBay board of directors to conduct a series of preliminary face-to-face interviews. The directors had chosen several finalists, and the next morning the board and the candidates were scheduled to board airplanes to travel to Menlo Park, California for final-round interviews. The question we were all debating: should we call off the meetings because of the pandemic, and if we weren't able to hold face-to-face interviews, what should we do?

The next morning, after the decision was made to call off the in-person interviews, we discussed what to do next. Should the board pause the CEO search entirely until it was safe to travel again, or should we shift the process to remote? One search committee member, who recognized the pandemic wasn't likely to be over quickly, reflected on the situation. "The next CEO is likely going to have to start remotely and lead in a virtual way well into the future. So we might as well shift the process so that we experience how the candidates will show up in a virtual setting the same way that our employees will."

That single comment brought into focus the golden rule of hiring, one we've reached during decades of experience conducting thousands of high-stakes executive searches: make sure the position specification reflects what is required to meet the *future* needs of the business and define and assess for those criteria, not what was needed in the past.

The shift to remote work is changing the talent market at all levels. When executive recruiters and company talent acquisition professionals talk with candidates about potential job changes, the most consistent deal breaker is the need to relocate. But as more companies embrace the ability to work from anywhere, relocation may become less necessary. Surveys conducted during the pandemic consistently show that many professionals no longer want to travel to an office five days a week, so companies that embrace all-remote or hybrid arrangements will increasingly be seen as more attractive employers. And at the executive level, in a world where more organizations embrace flexible work arrangements, there will be a premium placed on leaders who have successfully led a hybrid or fully virtual workforce or those who have the potential to effectively lead virtually.

A critical part of attracting great remote talent is showing the organization's comfort with working at a distance, and that starts by modeling a great virtual hiring process. While it may feel daunting to think about hiring someone without spending a lot of time together in person, or in some cases without ever meeting in person, we will share tips on how to run a highly effective virtual interview and recruiting process that will give you a reputation in the market as a go-to place for talent, that ensures you are hiring individuals capable of superior virtual leadership, and that yields benefits for your organization.

Create a Dynamic Profile That Reflects Your *Future* Needs

The foundation for any hiring process is defining the right profile and requirements. When considering virtual recruitment and leadership at a distance, the profile and requirements become even more important. In the recruiting world, we call this a "position specification."

When we work with boards on long-term CEO succession planning, the first step in the process is to build a CEO profile. This requires working with the board, CEO, and CHRO to define the current and evolving market and competitive context, assessing how well the company's strategy allows it to thrive in that context, and then articulating the professional experiences and leadership attributes necessary for that future scenario. We tell clients that a great profile is not something that is ever truly finished. It should be dynamic and revisited at least annually. Many hiring managers assume that when they complete a job profile, it is done and set in stone. But when the pandemic hit, many of our clients realized the impact would almost certainly shift the nature of their workforce and the strategic priorities for the next CEO. Accordingly, the boards we were working with immediately began revisiting their future CEO profiles, even if they had worked hard to develop them less than a year earlier.

One of our clients made changes (which are highlighted in bold below) to part of their future CEO profile to reflect the recognition that their next CEO would, in fact, need to lead a more virtual workforce:

- Genuine, authentic **and empathetic** leadership; builds trust and credibility
- Balanced intelligence (EQ/IQ); leads with both head and heart
- Guest and owner centricity; inclusive community mindset
- Action and results orientation; agent of change
- Adaptive learner
- Professional maturity; **cool**, calm **and collected under pressure**
- Gravitas and strong communicator; **the ability to communicate with purpose and clarity to inspire both in person and at a distance/remote**

If your organization is moving to hiring more virtual leaders, or if leading virtually will be an important aspect of the job going forward, it is critical to incorporate that changing reality into your profiles. In the next section we will cover some of the specific requirements for a great virtual leader, but the most important principle for any hiring decision is this: focus on the future. However, even once you've hired a great virtual leader, whether a CEO or manager, it is still important to revisit the profile annually and consider how the needs of your business context have changed. This is helpful not only to keep the hiring team focused on the right things, but it can also be a critical input to development planning to help your leaders and teams evolve with the changing context of your business.

Defining the Requirements: What Should I Look for in a Great Virtual Leader?

Okay, so you have taken stock of where your organization is going and have decided that you need more individuals capable of leading virtually. According to our research and observation, the most important characteristics for virtual leaders include strong communications and interpersonal skills, initiative, flexibility, and the ability to learn and adapt. Therefore, organizations should hire people who possess and excel on these dimensions.

Unfortunately, since virtual leadership is still a relatively new phenomenon, many hiring managers are not explicit about the fact that leading a virtual team is a challenging task and requires a different skill set than leading a traditional co-located team. Accordingly, when hiring a virtual leader, organizations should take the time to select the individual with the appropriate attributes – whether demonstrated experience or future potential – and not just assume that someone who has successfully led in a fully in-person environment will also be successful in a hybrid or fully remote leadership position.

If virtual leadership is one aspect and a key requirement of your future-oriented position specification, here are the key attributes to incorporate – both for virtual leaders and virtual team members:

A Successful Virtual Team Leader	A Successful Virtual Team Member
• Delegates work and responsibilities effectively; trusts others to achieve goals	• Demonstrates a high level of inherent motivation and proactivity
• Implements processes to effectively monitor work and hold people accountable (e.g., checks in without micromanaging, has strong project management skills)	• Effectively communicates with others (e.g., reaches out to others for help and proactively shares information with others)
• Effectively manages conflict	• Effectively collaborates with others
• Is comfortable working in an unstructured environment and can create clarity amid ambiguity	• Is comfortable working in an unstructured environment
• Demonstrates strong communication and leadership skills	• Can operate autonomously to achieve goals/objectives
• Inspires people to achieve results	• Is self-disciplined
• Effectively recognizes and rewards others	• Is proficient with technology
• Provides coaching and feedback to others and can adapt style to do this virtually	• Efficiently uses time and resources to carry out objectives
• Appropriately consults others when making decisions and fosters teamwork from a distance	• Resolves work-related problems quickly
• Demonstrates resilience	• Takes full accountability for decisions, actions, and performance

Walk the Talk: Virtual Interview Best Practices

When the eBay board made the decision to proceed with a virtual search for the next CEO in the middle of the pandemic, we revisited the interview process in its entirety. As the board director pointed out, the interview itself should reflect what it would be like for the candidate to interact with the board in a virtual environment, in addition to assessing how the candidate would lead his or her team and organization remotely.

As it turned out, all the finalist candidates and the entire eBay board were shocked by how positive the experience ultimately proved to be. They were delighted by the substantive quality of the interviews, which were in some cases better than meeting in person. The five members of the board's search committee met as a group with each of the five semi-finalist candidates on individual two-hour BlueJeans video meetings. After that, the full board met the three finalists during 90-minute videoconferences. By the end, directors felt that based on these virtual conversations, along with the executive assessments and deep reference checks that had been completed, they were *more* equipped to make the hiring decision than if the interviews had been conducted in person. Specifically, they noted that the nine-box grid view of the virtual screen, compared to seats around a typical rectangular board table, democratized the conversation in a way that both the candidates and the directors found valuable.

This emerging sense that video interviews can be not just as good as, but even better than, in-person interviews is not unique to hiring at the CEO level. Gerri Martin-Flickinger, chief technology officer of Starbucks, noted that in the nine months following the onset of the pandemic, they hired over 100 individuals into the tech organization completely virtually, and she believes they are better hires because of it.

What are some of the key factors the eBay board, Gerri, and others are relying on to lead such effective virtual interviews?

- **Rely on disciplined and objective criteria.** What we have seen from our own experience with many organizations is that something about being in person can lead to relying more on *feel* or *fit* than a systematically rigorous evaluation of how a candidate meets the criteria of the position specification. Gerri said this best: "Being virtual forces you to only focus on what the candidate is actually saying. Yes, it can feel like you are losing something by not being able to read body language as easily over Zoom, or that you are somehow not getting a full read of a person's 'style' or 'bearing.' But our experience is that interviewing virtually can actually promote more unbiased and objective evaluation of candidates. After Zoom interviews, we are less likely to receive feedback we too commonly hear, such as "I just got a better feeling from the first candidate than the second." When preparing for a virtual interview, or any interview, make sure the interviewers have the position specification and tailored questions to gather evidence for how the candidate has delivered results in the areas explicitly specified.

- **Use dynamic formats to gather additional data outside the interview.** Getting comfortable hiring someone without meeting them is admittedly difficult. But you can turn this into an advantage. In addition to creating a barrier to our own conscious or unconscious biases, being virtual gives you permission to gather more data and information in different formats. One concrete way to do this is to ask an interviewee something that would be impossible in an office setting. Ask them to show a framed photo or book on the bookshelf in their home office and then explain the significance or story behind it. You will be guaranteed to learn something about the person that would have never transpired in a traditional interview setting. In the wake of the financial crisis in 2008, Goldman Sachs[1] found itself in a war for talent with Silicon Valley and had to rethink both the type of talent they needed and how to assess for it. They developed asynchronous video interviews, where candidates record their answers to interview questions as part of a first round. The format leveled the playing field for candidates and allowed them to put their best foot forward. It also gave Goldman a digital library of data – and the ability to evaluate how candidates' answers correlated with their long-term performance on the job. Instead of just helping hire candidates today, that system gives Goldman the ability to study and reflect over time on how their process is working, and whether the questions and competencies they are testing for help in predicting success in the culture and at the firm. At Spencer Stuart, we use a variety of multi-method assessments that also bring data and objectivity to a hiring decision, all of which can be conducted virtually. Perhaps more importantly, assessments can help companies more accurately determine whether candidates have the preferences and capabilities to succeed in a virtual setting.

- **Thoughtful design and orchestration of the interview panel.** When interviewing an executive candidate in person, companies often spend thousands of dollars on travel to bring him or her to headquarters for back-to-back interviews. The people organizing the search struggle to find days when candidates and members of the interview panel can be in the office and available. Because of these logistical challenges, many interview panels ultimately get designed around one or two interviewers who are must-haves – and beyond that, recruiters are forced to add in whichever other interviewers are available on that day. Interviewing virtually reduces the randomness of availability; it allows you to create the *right* interview panels to get to the best answer. The interview panel should be diverse and include the hiring manager, a peer, a stakeholder, and the HR lead. Lori Goler, VP of People at Facebook, affirmed in our discussion that one of the biggest benefits of hiring virtually is breaking calendar logjam and moving the interview process along much more rapidly.

- **Set a facilitator and prep.** Once the panel has been determined, ensure there is someone designated as overall meeting facilitator, which includes responsibilities such as timekeeper and orchestrator of predesigned questions that each panelist would like to ask. Schedule time in advance for the panelists to prepare, align on desired outcomes, and define how post-interview decision-making will work. Some boards we work with divide up the interview questions ahead of time to maximize the time spent with each candidate and ensure coverage of key issues.

- **Tailored questions to assess virtual leadership.** As we specified earlier, what it takes to lead virtually requires some additional attributes to leading in person. An individual will need to excel in distinct areas. Accordingly, it is important to assess for those unique needs and make sure the questions you are asking will gather evidence in those areas. Our belief is that the most effective virtual leaders have exceptional communication and relationship-building skills. They are likely to demonstrate authenticity, empower others, and lead by example. While experience leading virtual teams is not necessarily a requirement, it is important that your hiring and assessment process emphasizes these important criteria. Some of the most powerful and proven interview questions can be tailored to factor in the virtual context. For example:

- Describe two accomplishments that you are especially proud of from the past year. How did you adapt your role in view of the pandemic and working remotely to achieve these milestones?

- What environments are most suited to you performing at your very best and in what contexts will you be frustrated and less effective? How have these changed since the onset of COVID-19?

- How have you changed your management style and approach to leading at a distance? What is working better for you and what is worse?

- **Good virtual interview etiquette will show the candidate you are equipped to support virtual leadership.** As mentioned above, the increase in remote work will make the war for talent more competitive, and organizations that are exemplars for virtual hiring will attract the best talent. How you show up as an interviewer and panel in the process will demonstrate to the candidates how equipped you really are to support them as a virtual leader. As we've stressed throughout this book, effective leadership in general and especially in a virtual world requires that you walk the talk. At a tactical level for interviewing, this means that you're looking into the camera, intentionally creating a warm personal connection up front, ensuring your technology and audio are working in advance, and doing all the same things you would expect of the candidate.

Virtual Hiring: A Net Benefit for All

"I've had no problem getting people to interview, no issue filling jobs, and I think we're hiring better people," said Gerri, the

Starbucks executive we've referred to throughout this chapter. "I see no downside to recruiting, interviewing, and hiring virtually."

Whether you believe remote working is net positive, net negative, or somewhere in the middle, adding a virtual element to your hiring process and incorporating some of the practices we shared will have significant advantages for your organization. Adapting your position specifications and profiles to be future oriented will increase the chances of selecting the right leader for your needs. Making at least a portion of your interview process more virtual will lower the stakes for both hiring managers and potential job seekers to start a conversation, lower the barrier to entry for those conversations, and give you access to better and more diverse candidates than ever before. Virtual hiring also has the obvious efficiency that the organization will reduce the number of in-person interviews it conducts, which reduces cost and increases speed.

For those organizations that are seeking to intentionally increase the percentage of their remote workforce and virtual leaders, adapting your hiring process in the ways that we have outlined will help you attract and select the best talent for the unique challenges of virtual leadership. Additionally, being more open to remote positions can increase access to a more diverse array of candidates, a critical imperative for the next generation of executives and a proven indicator of organizational outperformance. In the 2020 report from LeanIn.Org,[2] 70% of those surveyed believed that remote work will allow them to increase diversity in their hiring.

Finally, once you have successfully hired the best virtual leaders, the work does not stop there. Adapting your onboarding and tailoring the development and design of your teams to succeed virtually is critical for the retention and success of your leaders.

The Bottom Line

- Hiring someone for a virtual role – whether as a leader or as an employee – changes the specifications for the search. Employees who work remotely must be highly self-motivated and self-disciplined, comfortable with technology, able to collaborate easily, and comfortable with ambiguity. Leaders who manage remote teams must have high levels of trust, be able to check in and monitor work without micromanaging, and be exceptionally good at communication and coaching.

- Although video interviews take getting used to, they offer several benefits. They allow for more objectivity assessment than in-person interviews; they make it easier to schedule interviews, and it is easier to create higher-quality interview panels.

- Companies such as Starbucks and Facebook that have amassed experience hiring via video are convinced that they are seeing no drop in the quality of their hires – and in fact, they believe they are hiring a better and more diverse group of workers.

Notes

1 Dane E. Holmes, "Expanding the Pool," *Harvard Business Review*, May–June 2019, https://hbr.org/2019/05/expanding-the-pool?ab=seriesnav-spotlight.
2 Sarah Coury et al., "Women in the Workplace," McKinsey & Company, September 30, 2020, www.mckinsey.com/featured-insights/diversity-and-inclusion/women-in-the-workplace#.

8

Surviving Day One: A Toolkit for Remote Onboarding

In the tribal nations, of which there are more than 500 in the United States, it is customary for a new leader to shake the hand of every single person in a meeting, sometimes upward of 40 handshakes. The handshake symbolizes respect and the importance of community to the way they do business. Although the virtual world does not allow for physical handshakes, there is great value to creating a substitute ritual and maximizing the effect of the virtual greeting. This is especially important when introducing and onboarding new leaders. Appreciating this kind of symbolism and finding ways to re-create that moment virtually separate good virtual organizations from the great.

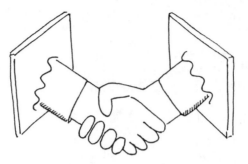

Most of the leaders we interviewed acknowledged that onboarding virtually is just plain hard. In our Virtual Experience survey, employee onboarding was cited as the single factor most negatively impacted by virtual work. In some ways, that is not that surprising. Some companies share a recording of their traditional, in-person onboarding program, or have executives duplicate the same sessions over live video. However, our research shows that this onboarding format will negatively impact an employee's experience. As Amgen CHRO, Lori Johnson, said in late 2020, "We saw a dip in satisfaction in our onboarding over the last nine months, so we've shifted our processes and have learned to use technology to allow us to use breakouts, dynamic whiteboards, and smaller group interactions, which have helped our onboarding experiences." It is this shift and restructuring that most organizations need to make.

Although onboarding does include some straightforward, logistical steps, such as setting up a new colleague's technology, providing access to systems, and acquainting the new person with key organizational processes, the more critical, make-or-break parts of onboarding are about:

1. Get off to a fast start.

2. Establish a foundation of strong relationships across the organization.

3. Explain the company culture and how work gets done.

4. Set clear expectations and connect the individual's work to the broader organizational mission, vision, and goals.

It turns out that the biggest barrier to creating an intentional, differentiated virtual onboarding experience is often mindset.[1] In the same way that it took television time to find the best ways to exploit the new medium (and grow beyond the earliest TV shows, which were really just radio shows with cameras), so too will companies need to develop onboarding programs that are tailored to the times and the technology. While most of this chapter will provide best practices for an effective, structured virtual onboarding experience for new employees across all levels, we have extensive experience in how organizations virtually onboard C-suite leaders and CEOs. There are specialized requirements for creating a transition and onboarding plan for a new CEO. In Jim's earlier book, *You're in Charge, Now What?*, we laid out a proven approach to help new leaders get off to a fast start in their first 100 days. The steps, which were developed based on studying the 100 best *and worst* CEO transitions, included aligning expectations between the CEO and a company's board of directors, the new CEO meeting and assessing the quality of the leadership team, crafting a strategic agenda to set the direction for the organization, communicating relentlessly to build the confidence amongst key internal and external stakeholders, taking actions to start to transform the culture, and avoiding the most common pitfalls (such as being a know-it-all and not letting go of one's previous identity).

Onboarding CEOs and Senior Executives

The key question is how to adapt these principles to a virtual world.

The section of *You're in Charge, Now What?* that has consistently received the most positive feedback was on the five questions a new CEO should pose to his or her team to create an agenda for active listening. The approach is as simple as it is powerful. In your first days as CEO, you send a note to the top 50 or even 100 leaders in your organization saying that you will be scheduling an hour-long one-on-one meeting to get their input on five key questions:

1. *What are the five most important things about the company we should be sure to preserve and why?*
2. *What are the top three things we need to change and why?*
3. *What do you most hope I do?*
4. *What are you most concerned I might do?*
5. *What advice do you have for me?*

Sending out these five questions ahead of time, and making it clear that the expectation is that each company leader should prepare their thoughts, allows the new CEO to listen as each person shares his or her views on these open-ended questions. Sitting quietly and listening isn't a habit of most CEOs, but it's a powerful technique. The new CEO can then analyze the results of the sessions, using this data as the foundation for the company's strategy and helping to shape a new CEO's actions throughout the first year.

Over the years, scores of new CEOs have told us that they have applied this approach for active listening. The results have been remarkable. Not only have those who have done this gotten great ideas and direction about how to lead their organizations, but they have often established new norms for engaging with, respecting, and soliciting the views of others. As a significant by-product of this process, when CEOs listened to what their executives thought, in a structured and encouraging way, they were able to quickly establish who were the thought leaders and potential change leaders of the organization and who were likely to be the blockers to the strategic and culture change agenda and needed to go.

The massive drawbacks to this approach, however, are time and logistics. To do 100 one-hour in-person meetings with a CEO's top leaders, especially in a global company, essentially became a full-time job for the first three months. Today, however, with the technical capability and cultural acceptance of video-conferences, a new leader can pursue this onboarding approach in a fraction of the time.

One new CEO, whom we'll call Melissa, did precisely this and then took this approach a couple of steps further. What started as her virtual onboarding plan has become her virtual leadership approach for the company on an ongoing basis.

Melissa started as CEO of a global industrial company in early 2020. The company needed a major turnaround financially, strategically, and culturally. These challenges were big enough on their own, but then COVID-19 set in and the company's revenue dropped by nearly 25%. To make matters worse, as the company's first externally appointed CEO, from an adjacent industry, and being the first woman CEO in the company's history, there was enormous resistance to her appointment.

Undeterred, Melissa was committed to building strong internal bridges, learning the organization, and creating trust, all while developing her turnaround plan. She had her assistant set up one-hour Microsoft Teams video meetings with the company's top 100 executives from around the world. She distributed a customized version of the five key questions for active listening and was able to get these meetings completed in just three (admittedly intensive) weeks. She identified themes about what should be changed and what should be preserved at the company. She gained a clear indication of who the company's thought leaders and influencers were. And she accelerated developing the foundation for the company's strategic and communications plans all while building relationships and trust with her team.

But then Melissa took this approach several steps further. First, she decided to create an *ongoing* schedule of video check-ins with her leaders on a rotating basis. Rather than having set meeting agendas and scheduling the calls for an hour, she also realized that scheduling for just a half hour and setting no agenda other than "How's it going?" was enormously powerful for gathering additional insights about the business and each executive's arena. A relationship-oriented leader, Melissa also kept careful notes from one conversation to the next and was able to reference back to ask about the health of an aging parent, or how a seventh grader was faring in school over Zoom. Finally, she realized that this management approach did not need to be limited to the company's top leaders. She could go direct and further down into and across the organization.

With the assistance of the company's CHRO, she put a list together of several hundred up-and-coming leaders and trusted functional experts from across the organization and had her assistant schedule check-in meetings with them too. The employees loved these personal connections. In her all-company meetings, Melissa was then able to share specific examples about who was doing what across the global enterprise. The CHRO reports that engagement scores from the pulse surveys have skyrocketed, and Melissa was seen as an authentic, empathetic, and accessible leader. Now a year into her CEO tenure, Melissa has adapted this remote leadership approach, which was forged from customizing her onboarding to the virtual world, even further. She came to realize that she didn't need even a half hour for these touch-base video calls. Fifteen minutes did the trick. Her assistant now keeps a database of all the people she speaks with and sets these 15-minute calls on an ongoing basis. Melissa told us she's never going back to the way she managed in the past.

Four General Onboarding Recommendations

Whether your organization creates individual onboarding plans or also leverages cohort-based onboarding, many of the same principles apply. The following sections explore these aforementioned recommendations:

1. Get off to a fast start.
2. Establish a foundation of strong relationships across the organization.
3. Explain the company culture and how work gets done.
4. Set clear expectations and connect the individual's work to the broader organizational mission, vision, and goals.

1. Get Off to a Fast Start

Think about the morning before your first day at your current company, or your first day at any new job. You probably didn't sleep well the night before. Your mind was spinning with anticipation, doubt, and uncertainty. This is probably especially true if you were starting a new job in the ambiguity of a virtual environment. The few moments of comfort that would typically present themselves in the early day – the quick bonding with a colleague in the hallway or being taken to lunch by your new boss or teammates – will not be available in a remote context.

It is also unlikely that a new employee joining your organization today has ever experienced a fully virtual onboarding process, since even companies with remote workforces frequently opted to do their onboarding in-person before the pandemic. With this sensitivity in mind, it is important to prepare for a remote onboarding before the new hire's first day. Create a plan to leverage a variety of strategies and interactions that can mitigate first-day nerves and allow your employee to feel welcome and gain confidence from the start.

Identify, Appoint, and Communicate a Dedicated Onboarding Liaison
In a nonvirtual world, having someone fill the role of informal mentor to support a new hire is a good idea, but it is even more critical remotely because the new leader won't have colleagues all around to ask questions as they come up. Creating a reliable, trusted channel for the new employee from the start will allow her to focus on absorbing new information and worry less about how and from whom to get questions answered.

It is important that the onboarding point of contact be a different person from the executive's manager, someone purposefully selected from the broader team or function, so that the new executive feels comfortable asking any questions, big or small. In the first few days of a new job even through the first year, any new employee will and *should* have endless questions on everything from technology and company strategy to culture and norms. The last thing you want is having your new leader feel uncertain about who to ask a question to or, even worse, questioning whether she should even ask a certain question at all. The dedicated onboarding liaison will not have all the answers but should have a deep knowledge of the organization so that he or she can direct any of the new hire's questions accordingly.

Prior to the first day, the onboarding liaison should proactively reach out to welcome the new employee, provide an overview of her schedule for the first week, and establish him or herself as the new individual's go-to person when something's not working, or if she is not sure who to go to for something. Todd Billingsley, director of leadership and business development at Boehringer Ingelheim, observed in our conversation that check-ins drive positive engagement by more than 15%, so once the executive has started, consider creating a quick daily standup at the end of each day or week to field any outstanding questions from the day or to plan for how to direct unanswered questions.

Create a Connection to the Company Before Day One   As soon as any new employee, from entry level manager to the CEO, agrees to come on board and a start date has been set, find an opportunity to make the new employee feel a part of the family. New employees are often at the peak of emotional openness and feelings of positivity to the company right before they start, so use the opportunity to cement the connection to the soon-to-start employee. Reckitt Benckiser, now known as RB, the global consumer products company, sends a care package to employees' homes before their start date, complete with a selection of the company's cleaning, health, and hygiene products. While many companies do this, and they absolutely should, what makes the RB onboarding package especially powerful is how they use it as an opportunity to reinforce the mission and values of the company. In addition to the array of Dettol, Lysol, Finish, and Air Wick products included in the box, RB also encloses a note:

> *Congratulations on your new role and joining RB. We all welcome you and look forward to your successful journey with us. At RB, we exist to protect, heal and nurture in the relentless pursuit of a cleaner and healthier world. We fearlessly innovate in this pursuit across our Hygiene, Health and Nutrition businesses. We have a fight on our hands. A fight to make access to the highest quality*

*hygiene, wellness and nourishment a right and not a privilege.
For everyone. Everywhere. It's a big ambition and we're determined to make it happen. Welcome aboard. Together we will create
a cleaner, healthier world.*

Set Up Technology Ahead of the Start Date   Another practical
tip for helping your new leader enter their first day with
confidence is to set up their technology ahead of the start date.
Prepare and send them a company-issued laptop and phone with
all the security protocols and customized software. Then have a
session before day one with a company expert and liaison to show
how the platforms operate, including the videoconferencing
platform, communications channels, and other company systems.
Simulating the experience and troubleshooting any potential
technology and communications issues prior to the first day will
allow your new employee to be fully present and comfortable on
their first day. If issues do arise, she will have a familiar face to
help her navigate.

Rosie Allan, senior director of Talent Management, Learning and Culture at FINRA, recalls how their organization created "FINRA in a Box," which gets physically delivered to a new
employee's residence prior to their first day. It includes "essential items such as a laptop, onboarding instructions, introductory materials, branded merchandise – and even a few pieces of
candy to sweeten their first day," she says. "Not only is it logis-
tically beneficial, but culturally as well. People post about the
delivery on social media, and it helps build camaraderie and
showcase our values."

Just as we identified value adds of virtual hiring and assessing for able virtual leaders, a seamless technological experience
aids in a company's ability to drive to more effective outcomes
from a new leader more quickly.

Facilitate an Informal Check-In Between the New Leader, Their Manager, and a Small Community Generally, before a new hire starts, whether remotely or not, all the interactions she's had up until that point with her manager have been part of the interviewing or negotiation phases. A critical part of helping your new executive get off to a strong start is helping her to build trust and rapport with her manager. Early touch points between the new leader and her manager can give the new hire more confidence and establish early open lines of communication. Because sitting in a remote setting can feel isolating, encourage one or two other individuals in the organization to connect with the new executive ahead of starting so that the individual enters the first day with an already-developing sense of community.

2. Establish a Foundation of Strong Relationships across the Organization

In the onboarding phase, it is best to invest in even more frequent and varied interactions between the leader, key stakeholders, and teammates up front than you would during traditional, in-person onboarding. In a virtual setting, you can't rely as much on the organic and spontaneous relationship-building that happens in hallways, over lunches, and at office events. That's why it's best to be proactive and intentional about setting up a mix of formal and informal one-on-one interactions between the new hire and other individuals. Additionally, it is important to organize a mix of different group discussions so that the new hire can develop contextual understanding of team dynamics. Lastly, one risk of virtual work is that it can make it easy for an individual or leader to operate in silos or with the same network of people on a regular basis. Creating both a strong core network and a broader network across the organization will allow the executive to be more successful long term.

Organizations using cohort-based onboarding programs are often blending a series of informal and formal experiences for people to learn new skills as well as build relationships. At MetLife, which uses an apprenticeship model for both new hires as well as for peer learning and development, CHRO Susan Podlagar and CEO Michel Khalaf shared that they brought 3,000 leaders in for mandatory training on maintaining connections with new hires, creating community, and building in touchpoints, even while working at a distance. The key to making an apprenticeship *and to building capabilities for leadership at all levels* work remotely, they say, is to act with intentionality. Luckily, using the virtual classroom and other technologies can be a great way to replicate the experience of bringing people together in person. Organizations will need to be even more mindful of how to create an engaging onboarding journey for new employees, perhaps over the course of their first year.

Build Strong 1:1 Relationships Because the new hire is onboarding virtually, she may feel like she is missing out on small talk that naturally occurs when meeting someone for the first time in person. It can also be harder for the new hire to build an understanding of each person's role and how she fits into the broader team. To combat both challenges, encourage your new hire and their teammates to set up a mix of formal conversations to cover roles, responsibilities, and business objectives and shorter, informal interactions over coffee, lunch, or debriefing on a recent meeting. Encourage the new hire and individuals they are meeting with to take a few minutes at the start of either type of discussion to do a personal warm-up.

Just as in the case of virtual interviewing, one of the advantages of virtual onboarding is the general availability of colleagues to meet over video. It will be easier for new hires to get meetings scheduled with colleagues. Because authenticity is especially important in a virtual environment, the more that new hires take the opportunity to tell their full stories in a highly personal way, the more committed their new colleagues will be to their success. So encourage your new employees to proactively set up introductory video chats with a wide array of colleagues and then encourage them to tell their full stories in these meetings. Equally importantly suggest that they do the same and ask their more seasoned colleagues to share their personal journeys as well. There will be plenty of time for working the formal business agenda later, but you only have one chance to create a favorable first impression.

Recognize Team Dynamics and Build a Broader Network

Research[2] shows that it is more powerful to have a broad network than a deep network, especially as one becomes increasingly senior in an organization. All employees need to create effective working relationships with colleagues who can help them get their jobs done. However, as individuals grow from management into leadership roles, their networks must be expanded to include broader and, in some cases, external relationships to have the most accurate view of the future and resources to help their organizations succeed. When a new leader onboards, the organization should help him or her intentionally build a broad network, starting internally. While one-on-one meetings are powerful for establishing foundational relationships and trust and rapport, having your new hire begin sitting in on group discussions from day one can help them put individuals into the context of how work gets done at the organization and to get exposure to a broader set of people and stakeholders.

During the first few months of a new hire's onboarding, consider setting up a shadow week in which the new hire attends a wide variety of team and stakeholder group meetings, even those who may feel less directly relevant to that new hire's core responsibilities. Also, encourage the new hire to proactively reach out to people across the company to get to know people they may not otherwise come across. At Facebook, we learned in our conversations that onboarding used to typically be driven and managed by an onboarding team, but in a virtual environment, the responsibility was broadened to not just the onboarding team and the manager, but also to one's peers through the increased use of internal resources such as Facebook affinity groups and employee resource groups.

When we spoke to Dominique Taylor, chief people officer at the digital media company Axios, she mentioned that the organization found the ability to ensure consistent varied interactions of both new hires and employees across the firm so valuable that they implemented Donut, a "slack robot" that uses the messaging platform Slack to randomly assign new hires to have "virtual donuts and coffee" together with another employee from across the organize once a month. At Axios, this ritual continues long after an employee has "finished" onboarding. Throughout their tenure, everyone (including the CEO) has virtual donuts and coffee with someone new from across the organization once a month.

3. Explain the Company Culture and How Work Gets Done

While we will cover more about building culture virtually and understanding cultural styles of new hires in Chapter 10, it is imperative to walk and talk about the company's culture from the onset. Spend more time than you generally would in a face-to-face environment talking about what is typical and atypical across various cultural dimensions. Create the space for your new colleagues to ask about the way things are done as well.

Make Unspoken Assumptions Explicit   Many organizations rely on organic ways of communicating shared history and norms. Whether virtually or not, memorializing a company's history in videos, in the About Us section on the website, and in documents can help accelerate a process that may otherwise take longer to capture over a series of many interactions with long-standing members of the organization. Additionally, as awkward as it may seem, it can be helpful to create explicit guidance and communication around norms that are often taken for granted – the company's tone and level of formality, dress code, virtual etiquette on videoconferences, messaging norms, and working hours. Leaving someone to observe, guess, and adapt to these norms on their own can create unnecessary ambiguity and stress.

Designate a Culture Buddy   Even if you are successful at codifying and sharing more explicit information about your company's history, culture, and norms when onboarding virtually or having employees work across a variety of different locations, it doesn't ensure new hires pick up on all of them. Even when companies try, it's still harder for new hires to pick up on cultural cues and the distinct unwritten rules of the team and the broader organization that make someone feel like a part of the culture and community.

Assigning a culture buddy – a particular form of mentor – creates a trusted relationship for your new hire to ask questions and get feedback and direction on how they can be most effective understanding and adapting to culture dynamics. Key activities of a culture buddy include debriefing after meetings or making quick one-on-one calls after an important group discussion to help the new hire get a read on informal dynamics. A culture buddy can also help the new hire identify their strengths that complement the culture and flag how certain actions could be perceived negatively by others. New employees can use that information during the transition to understand the key attributes of the culture and how their style may be viewed by others. Often, just understanding the key elements of the culture can make a tremendous difference in a new hire's ability to be successful.

4. Set Clear Expectations and Connect the Individual's Work to the Broader Organizational Mission, Vision, and Goals

A new hire should have a clear picture of what success looks like for the first 100 days and beyond. New hires should recognize how their responsibilities fit into the overall success of the company. When an individual joins the company, the hiring manager should share key communications and presentations that have been done by the leadership of the organization on the near-term and longer-term direction and goals of the company so that the new hire can put their work into the context of the whole.

As part of developing a 100-day plan, we advise new CEOs to develop and test their hypotheses about strategy and key priorities with members of the team, rather than presenting their plan to their team and the organization at large. No one wants to follow someone who believes that they must be the smartest person in the room. Even if you do happen to possess all the answers as a new employee – which you almost never do – it is far more effective to develop your views about direction and priorities in an iterative, shared manner. This is especially applicable in a virtual environment, where a new leader needs to seek all opportunities to build trust, gain buy-in, and achieve alignment early on.

As the new hire is getting up to speed, having a clear set of responsibilities and outcomes can be critical to helping them prioritize and sequence their work and accomplish some quick wins that create a strong foundation and momentum for the individual's future success. Over the long term, while a role can evolve, adapt, and become more complex and ambiguous, having clarity from the start will create a foundation from which the individual can more readily adapt.

Conclusion

Onboarding is one of the most important drivers of employee success. Getting off to a strong start creates momentum from which to build and accelerate. Getting off to a poor start breaks a new employee's confidence and leads the organization to question the wisdom of the hire. While it can be hard to imagine recreating a fun and memorable onboarding program that can live up to what you may traditionally do in person, there are many benefits that technology unlocks through virtual onboarding.

What separates the firms that do onboarding best, inclusive of being virtual, is that the work is intentional, and it does not end after the first week, first 30 days, or even the first 100 days. Your onboarding program should just be the beginning of an ongoing development foundation that continues to strengthen your employees' cultural alignment, relationships across your organization, and performance in their role.

The Bottom Line

- Virtual onboarding is challenging and a top priority for leaders. It requires making new employees feel supported and set up for success, helping them to form relationships, understand the culture, and set clear expectations. This is harder to do virtually and requires more ongoing effort.

- Some organizations assign new employees an onboarding liaison so that new hires have a dedicated person to reach out to (besides their new boss), and a "culture buddy" to help them understand the company's unwritten rules and norms.

- It is particularly important to find ways to increase informal interaction for new hires (over the first year) so that they are not solely responsible for this. Start by creating a list of key relationships each new hire will need to build, and schedule one-on-one coffee or lunch meetings by video.

Notes

1 Mary Driscoll and Michael D. Watkins, "Onboarding a New Leader – Remotely," *Harvard Business Review*, May 18, 2020, https://hbr.org/2020/05/onboarding-a-new-leader-remotely.

2 Herminia Ibarra and Mark Lee Hunter, "How Leaders Create and Use Networks," *Harvard Business Review Magazine*, January 2007, https://hbr.org/2007/01/how-leaders-create-and-use-networks.

9

Continuous Improvement: High-Impact Coaching and Accountability at a Distance

At Boehringer-Ingelheim (BI), the German-based pharmaceutical giant, district managers typically spend a full day riding along with each sales rep every quarter, sitting in as they meet with physicians and other customers. Watching the reps do their actual job of selling allows managers to observe behavior and provide in-the-moment coaching as soon as they leave the doctor's office together. In normal times, the typical district manager spends 80 or 100 days a year in the field, helping coach reps to sell and engage more effectively.

When COVID-19 hit, the way BI coaches its reps had to change. In-person ride-alongs were out. Instead, "managers have converted their traditional half-day in-person coaching into a series of virtual coaching sessions to provide feedback and coaching," says Todd Billingsley, BI's director of leadership and business development. District managers also began hosting virtual coaching office hours to discuss best practices, help convey a sense of purpose, and demonstrate what good looks like. In addition to managing the logistics of shifting their coaching practices to video, BI also had to reconsider how it measures the coaching performance of district managers, since traditional metrics (such as the number of days spent in the field with reps) were no longer relevant. But whether the conversations take place on video or at a socially distant meeting outside in a park, the company is emphatic that coaching must remain a vital part of day-to-day life.

Many leaders we work with experience challenges providing meaningful coaching – they aren't quite sure how to do it, how to add value, or even what posture to take. In a virtual environment, coaching can be more difficult. The good news is that research[1,2] shows that online coaching is as effective as in-person coaching, but it does take a focused effort. In our Virtual Experience survey, mentorship and career development were among the top challenges reported, along with dealing with conflict and motivating employees. Similarly, in a pulse survey in 2020 at the media measurement giant Nielsen, amidst a surge in positive engagement scores, the metric that decreased was "My manager has checked in with me." As Nielsen CEO David Kenny acknowledged when we spoke, "Managers need to build in time to check in with their people. The informal office check-ins have disappeared, so both the givers and receivers of coaching have to change and do things differently."

Boeing CEO David Calhoun concedes that you may lose something by not being face to face, but he has made up for this by increasing the frequency of coaching he's done. "There is no substitute for being in person to deliver feedback and development advice, but I've found that having more frequent touch points, which I like to do on FaceTime, compensates and works well."

Recently, we were coaching a senior leader at a global manufacturing company who was used to seeing his direct reports in the office each week. He took pride in talking informally about what his team members were working on and finding little openings to let him offer nuggets of advice. Working remotely, he needed to shift his approach. He had to become far more intentional and disciplined to find the time for these conversations, create enough space for catch-up conversations, and *then* find the specific hooks on which to hang his coaching advice. By setting up weekly check-ins and planning each video meeting in advance, he is now making equal or even greater progress guiding his team.

We introduced the concept of using virtual coaching exercises with Pat, a leader we were advising. Pat was working with a direct report who was trying to inspire people to make an important change. We showed Pat how to leverage Miro, an online collaborative platform, to visually whiteboard and help "walk" people through the situation. Once Pat learned how to use the tool, he conducted an interactive session using Miro (see Figure 9.1) to conduct an analysis of why this particular change was needed, identify the requirements for this change, as well as envision the future state. As Pat and his team member brainstormed together during the coaching dialogue, they filled out digital Post-it notes during a highly interactive session. This simple technique was effective at helping Pat's team member successfully plan for and

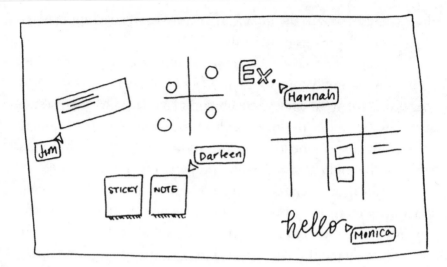

FIGURE 9.1

communicate a critical organizational change. The same technique can be applied for activities such as brainstorming, collaborative problem-solving, or creating an action plan.

This chapter is all about how to coach effectively at a distance. This requires that you identify and apply the skills for remote coaching and to ensure accountability. Since coaching and managing accountability are highly intertwined, we will cover both here. Keep in mind that coaching and holding people accountable are *skills*. Just like chess, tennis, or cooking, developing your ability to coach and hold people accountable is a skill that will be developed through focus and disciplined practice. And applying these skills with people who are not with you in person requires specialized tactics.

What is it about the virtual environment that makes coaching more challenging? First, active listening skills become even more essential due to the decreased ability to read visual cues or body language. Individuals' behavior over video can be more artificial, which can make accurate interpretation more difficult.

As a result, it is more important for a leader to consistently use strong active listening skills such as paraphrasing, empathizing, and responding to others in a balanced way.

Certain communication channels distort the tone of one's message. Research has found that there is a negativity bias in the perception of the email tone. Emails perceived to be neutral by the sender are often perceived as negative by the recipients. Emails perceived by senders to be positive in tone tend to be considered only neutral by recipients. As a result, email and text are not the media of choice for coaching and providing feedback. Surprisingly, many leaders do this, and it creates unintended problems.

Another common concern among leaders is that there may be fewer opportunities to observe performance and deliver feedback in a timely manner, which can lead to a lack of clarity regarding expectations. Dominique Taylor, chief people officer at the digital media company Axios, mentioned a similar anxiety about whether employees would be as productive in a virtual environment. The team quickly reframed the question from focusing on the input – hours working in the office – to the outputs. "We realized that if we are meeting our goals and creating the right levels of production with our quality standards, then yes, our people are working well," she said. The senior leadership reminded themselves that they had consistently hired highly motivated and disciplined professionals, so they didn't need to worry about over-observation.

In the virtual environment, leaders need to be ready to address issues including isolation, anxiety, and problems with work-life balance. Furthermore, these issues might go undetected for a long period of time, resulting in negative outcomes such as decreased productivity and engagement, even depression.

A helpful tactic is to consider the location of your check-ins. Despite not being in an office to coach someone, it can be beneficial to select your physical location as well as the other person's location to create the best setting for a quality discussion. One CEO we coach takes walks on the beach when having important – and sometimes tough – discussions. She encourages others to get away from their desks so that they can focus on the conversation. Everyone has witnessed ineffective managers multitasking during feedback conversations or other important discussions, and this, of course, negatively impacts the outcome. A key to effective coaching is being focused, in-the-moment, and fully engaged with the person with whom you are speaking. It may be helpful to schedule time in your calendar to prepare for a coaching discussion to ensure that it is high impact.

We believe the skills strong coaches deploy are foundational to providing feedback and exploring solutions. When it comes to the best-in-class virtual coaches, they adapt their behavior and approach to reflect the nuances of a virtual setting, and they work at it.

Principles of Virtual Coaching

Whether in person or via a video call, the fundamentals of coaching don't change. Highly effective virtual coaches consistently do the following:

- **Build trust.** This is perhaps the most critical component for leadership and high-impact coaching (see Chapter 2 on building trust).

- **Balance a focus on task and relationships.** Do not make assumptions – provide context and solicit input before going into problem-solving mode.

- **Let the person feel heard.** When providing advice, encourage the other person to respond – and when they do, listen closely.

- **Ask good questions.** Increase the use of both open-ended and specific questions to solicit feedback and confirm understanding. Use effective questions to make up for a potential lack of visual cues.

There are five important skills that help leaders operationalize the principles of virtual coaching. We will review each briefly since they are the foundation for success, especially when coaching virtually.

Skill 1: Paraphrasing

To overcome the lack of visual cues on video calls, the proactive and consistent use of paraphrasing is an example of the change in behavior that effective virtual leaders make. Simply put, paraphrasing is restating what you heard the other person say in your own words. This skill is always important, but in a virtual world, it is essential. Seventy percent of the information we process in interpersonal communication is through nonverbal communication.[3] Fewer visual cues increase the likelihood of miscommunication, especially on global or cross-cultural teams where people's native languages or societal contexts are different. The benefit of paraphrasing is that it shows that you understand, but do not necessarily agree with, what the other person said. If you disagree with what the person said, it is important to restate what you think the person said and confirm your understanding before stating your own point of view.

A few tips on paraphrasing well:

- Do not show approval or disapproval and avoid parroting the person (using his or her exact words).
- Work hard to understand the other person's point of view (rather than planning your rebuttal). Or, as the late, great

management guru Stephen Covey wrote as habit 5 in *The 7 Habits of Highly Effective People*, "Seek first to understand, then be understood."[4]

- If you disagree, restate the other person's point of view before stating your own.

Skill 2: Empathizing

While paraphrasing focuses on the content of what someone has said, empathizing focuses on how someone is *feeling*. Empathizing is the primary way we connect with people in the physical world, and it is even more important in a virtual environment. Empathizing demonstrates that you understand the other person's situation. It does not necessarily mean that you agree or that you feel the same way. Empathy meets someone where they are. Kathleen Hogan, CHRO at Microsoft, described their approach as Model-Coach-Care. "Care doesn't mean you have to be my best friend," she said, "but care means it's important to know the individual situation of an employee when providing coaching. Does she have five kids and how is she dealing with that stress?" Empathy, in other words, starts by caring to know about the individual.

A few tips on empathizing:

- Watch for the nonverbal as well as the verbal message. It is especially important to probe when the nonverbal message is inconsistent with the verbal message.
- Respond by being patient and nonjudgmental. Paraphrase back to acknowledge the emotional component of the message.
- Do not interrupt. Let people speak and, especially if they are upset, let them vent. People are less likely to be hostile or resistant if they feel that they are being listened to.

- Overcome the urge to ignore, disagree with, or reject what a person says.
- Try not to be "efficient." It is difficult to be genuinely empathetic if you're on a tight schedule or thinking that the conversation is something you must tick off your to-do list.

Skill 3: Questioning

We have facilitated hundreds of sessions with leaders across industries to help enhance their ability to coach. One of the most common mistakes that we see is when leaders inadvertently ask close-ended questions, which shuts down a dialogue. The main point of using questions when coaching is to gather information and to clarify what someone is saying. Often, effective questioning lets the other person come to the best conclusion themselves, helping them take full ownership. Questioning can also help guide the conversation and encourage two-way dialogue. In addition, questioning can help you take the measure of the other person or help you understand what they know and how they would approach the problem. Finally, it helps uncover gaps in their thinking so you can better determine what you need to coach.

A few tips on asking questions to uncover information:

- Use open-ended questions, such as "What do you think?" or "How did it make you feel?"
- Ask questions that encourage "How can we?" thinking.
- Avoid asking questions that put people on the defensive (for example, "Why did you . . . ?" "Why didn't you . . . ?").
- Avoid leading questions (for example, "Don't you agree that . . . ?").
- Do not ask, "Do you understand?" to check for understanding.

- Expand your open-ended question to ask about mental health and work-life balance in a way that won't make them feel uncomfortable. (For example, "There is so much going on in the world right now. How are you doing with everything at the moment?")

Skill 4: Focusing on Behavior

This is the most overlooked part of coaching, especially when leaders are vague when providing feedback. When discussing performance or offering coaching, clear communication means being specific and focusing on the person's behavior or actions, rather than on attitude or personality, which is likely to provoke defensiveness. Let's take a close look at why this is important.

Coaching and feedback are more effective when they are directed toward things people have control over and can change. Focusing on behavior refers to how the specific actions impact others or the environment. In one example, a board director we know noticed a fellow director's views being undervalued because he used verbal crutches (such as "you know," "I mean," and "right") so frequently when he spoke that it became distracting. When she pointed it out, the fellow director was surprised because he hadn't even heard himself doing it. So, with his permission, she started keeping hash marks during board meetings to count how many times he used those words. In one meeting it was over 75 times! He was shocked. She kept doing this at subsequent board meetings and it became a bit of a bond between the two. Importantly, that awareness helped him dramatically reduce this verbal tic. Another example: If you're trying to coach someone to be more consistent in project planning, be clear that when they do not provide updates on project milestones, it creates bottlenecks for the others on the team who are relying on that information. When coaching, focusing on the impact of specific behaviors helps the individual see the broader importance of addressing those behaviors.

To ensure you are focusing on the person's behavior, follow these steps:

- When you identify an issue that seems attitudinal, ask yourself, "What did the person *do* or *say* that indicated that he has a bad attitude, procrastinates, is uncooperative?" Or what does the person do that diminishes their gravitas or makes them less effective? Keep asking the question until you isolate the offending behavior.
- Identify the specific changes that address the behavior. If it is something inherent that cannot be changed, that is obviously not an area for coaching.

Skill 5: Using a Balanced Response Technique

Let's paint a picture of a common challenge that leaders face when coaching others, which is exacerbated in a virtual setting. Sally, who is your direct report, often comes to you with ideas for new strategies or innovative approaches. While Sally is creative and you welcome her ideas, you often do not have the budget to implement them relative to other priorities, or in some cases the idea is not practical given the business climate. You don't want to shut Sally down, and you consistently must give her this feedback. Another example is your direct report, Paul, who is a Type-A personality and gets defensive any time you provide feedback to enhance his performance. So what should you do?

A balanced response is a technique for providing constructive feedback about someone's behavior, performance, an idea, or proposal without being confrontational or diminishing his or her self-esteem. It is about giving others information on what they are doing effectively – performance and behaviors – and on what they can do differently to be more effective or to improve performance. Here is how to use it when coaching:

- First, state what you like about a person's performance or idea – the positives. Examples:

  "What I like about your idea is . . ."
  "The strengths are . . ."
  "What I found particularly effective/helpful/useful is . . ."

- Then, state your concerns about performance or ideas in actionable, "how-to" form. Examples:

  "What I'm concerned about your decision on (task/project) is . . ."
  "How can we overcome (the barriers that keep idea from being acceptable)?"
  "I wish we could . . ."

Sometimes a challenging conversation is actually better done virtually. Carol Tomé, CEO of delivery giant UPS, says she's recognized that being outside of the office makes it feel safer to address sensitive topics over video. In the office someone might overhear a conversation or observe body language in a glass-walled conference room and employees may be naturally more guarded. But be sensitive about the technology and try to adapt your approach to the person and situation. Even as people complain about "Zoom burnout," coaching is best done live, even if that's on video. Text and chat are useful for quick check-ins, and email is fine to summarize discussions and action plans, but live communications are essential to deliver coaching.

Managing Accountability

Many virtual leaders find accountability challenging, especially true if they are leading matrixed or project teams in which team members report to someone else. EPAM Co-Head of Global Business Balazs Fejes noticed that when working remotely, sharing data led to an enhanced desire from the team to contribute toward goals, because it created more transparency. It is easier for people to act with lower levels of accountability in a virtual setting, and we will discuss this further shortly. Fejes's colleague, EPAM CMO and Head of Strategy Elaina Shekhter, points out that people don't learn how to do this naturally – it requires training. Without training, people will have a hard time adapting to virtual leadership, and Shekhter sees the success of this training as a differentiator between companies going forward.

A common view of being accountable is that it is admitting mistakes or, more often, determining whose fault it is when performance declines, problems develop, or results are not delivered. That's only part of accountability. In addition, people who are accountable take the initiative to ensure problems get solved and projects are completed on time.

When people shift to remote work, meeting deadlines and quality standards are more important than when, where, and how many hours people work. In addition, different metrics might be necessary to measure performance, because virtual team member contributions are often less visible and because some team members may not be carrying their fair load – a phenomenon known as "social loafing." Social loafing increases when there are low levels of identifiability – that is, when it is more difficult to connect individual actions to a specific outcome. We will discuss how to deal with this when we review the tools for managing accountability.

Let's start by looking at three common accountability mistakes that virtual leaders make.

Mistake 1: Not clearly communicating who will be held accountable for what.

It is almost impossible to hold someone accountable if you have not clarified expectations. Effective virtual leaders ensure that each commitment is tied to a specific person and that responsibilities are clearly outlined.

Mistake 2: Agreeing on an action, but not setting a completion date.

We know people are busy and under stress, and we may hesitate to add to the pressure by specifying a due date, so we say, "As soon as possible." Unfortunately, failing to specify a deadline increases the likelihood of projects running late. It is better to set clear, ambitious, but realistic deadlines. You can't hold people accountable if you haven't set clear expectations about next steps linked with a due date. If you shirk from doing so, the conversation then becomes one of "you said/they said," and both parties would be correct. Beyond setting the completion date, a manager must set a check-in on that date. Often, managers are hesitant to enforce agreed-on completion dates because they don't want to be seen as tough to work with, or they want their employees to like them. Similarly, many virtual leaders are hesitant to monitor progress because they are concerned that checking in will be perceived as micromanaging or communicate a lack of trust. As a result, they often learn about missed deadlines or delays when it is too late. But employees – and especially high performers – appreciate clarity and being held to task. The old saying that "As a manager, it's better to be respected than liked" can be a good mantra for you as a leader when it comes to accountability.

Mistake 3: Not holding people accountable for missed commitments after the fact.

Even though many virtual leaders would rather ignore performance problems, doing so has negative consequences. First, it creates a tone that it is acceptable to do shoddy work or miss set deadlines. Second, when performance problems are not addressed, they are, of course, more likely to keep occurring. If you wait to address a problem, it becomes even more difficult down the road because previous situations were ignored. Finally, some of the barriers to execution that led to the missed deadline or commitment are likely to remain in place. Discussing problems and obstacles that impede performance as soon a performance problem arises helps prevent the same issues from popping up again in the future.

Setting People Up for Success

The best way to manage accountability is to ensure people follow through in the first place, versus trying to get someone to be accountable after someone dropped the proverbial ball. The acronym ATC (short for "air traffic control") can help:

Action – Use action plans and team project management sites to clarify expectations and who is accountable. There are project management sites like Basecamp, Trello, Asana, and Zoho, and many organizations use Microsoft Teams to track progress on projects or deliverables.

Timetable – This defines who will do what by when. It sounds basic but commitments that do not have a time frame

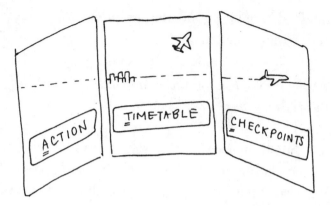

usually fall by the wayside. This is even more critical when working virtually.

Checkpoints – This means completing a progress check *before* the completion date.

Many virtual leaders fail to use this third technique, because they often believe that to check in on progress suggests a lack of confidence in a direct report. To avoid this, ask about progress in a way that communicates the assumption that the action was completed: "How did the meeting go? What worked and what obstacles did you encounter?" is a more trusting and far more effective way to start the discussion.

After-the-Fact Accountability Booster: Three Coaching Questions

When used effectively, three coaching questions encourage people to take accountability for their actions and consequences. These questions can be used after the fact when a commitment is missed, as well as during checkpoint meetings. These questions turn the act of managing accountability into a coaching intervention (hence the interconnectedness of coaching and managing accountability). You can use the questions to increase accountability if someone has failed to deliver – but remember, prevention is better than an after-the-fact fix. Coach the other person to ask himself or herself these questions nondefensively:

- Past: "What could I have done to prevent the problem? What, if anything, did I do that might have possibly contributed to the problem?"
- Present: "What can we do now to get things back on track?"
- Future: "What can I do to prevent this problem from happening again in the future?"

In our experience, leaders understand the foundational skills necessary to effectively coach and hold people accountable in a virtual setting. However, we consistently see leaders make mistakes and revert to old tendencies when working remotely. We suggest that you start by focusing on implementing a few of the best practices we outlined until they become a habit.

The Bottom Line

- Managers who excel at coaching use paraphrasing, empathizing, and good questions to show they are listening closely, and provide balanced feedback in a timely manner, despite the distance. Excelling at this in a virtual environment requires superior communication skills.
- In a virtual setting, leaders need to be less focused on when people work and instead focus on deliverables and outcomes. This may require a mindset shift but is especially important to foster a culture of empowerment and trust.

- Remote work sometimes leads to "social loafing." This is particularly true when large groups are involved in project work, which creates a form of anonymity: everyone's contribution may be hard to separate from the larger team, leading people to slack off. Manage this by setting clear roles and checking in individually to ask people if team members' contributions are equitable.

Notes

1 R.M. Berry et al., "A comparison of face-to-face and distance coaching practices: Coaches' perceptions of the role of the working alliance in problem resolution," *Consulting Psychology Journal: Practice and Research* 63:4 (2011): 243–253, https://doi.org/10.1037/a0026735

2 Joshua Tompkins, "Money for Nothing? The Problem of the Board-Exam Coaching Industry," *New England Journal of Medicine* 365:2 (July 14, 2011).

3 Dustin Smith, "Nonverbal Communication: How Body Language & Nonverbal Cues Are Key," lifesize (blog), February 18, 2020, www.lifesize.com/en/blog/speaking-without-words/.

4 Steven R. Covey, "The 7 Habits of Highly Effective People", Franklin Covey, Accessed March 5, 2021, www.franklincovey.com/the-7-habits/habit-5/.

10

The Culture Conundrum: Building and Sustaining Culture Virtually

In our leadership advisory work, culture comes up constantly – as it did in our interviews for this book. Perhaps not surprisingly, our survey findings show that only 20% of respondents felt that the virtual shift has had a positive impact on company culture, 43% thought that it has had a negative impact, and 38% were neutral. Given the importance of culture, many leaders mentioned culture as a top priority in this virtual shift.

Peter Drucker famously said, "Culture eats strategy for breakfast." While this quote is so well known it can be considered conventional wisdom, there is actually some dispute[1] as to whether Drucker actually said this. The fact is that there are no actual citations to this in his extensive writing. We can assure you here, however, that he did say it! At least he said it to Jim, when Jim interviewed him for his 1998 book, *Lessons from the Top*. Beyond that morsel of business trivia, the important point is that culture is both important and has a massive influence on organizational and individual performance.

Despite the growing appreciation for the importance of culture, few executives can describe what drives their organization's culture or whether their culture supports or works against the strategic priorities of the business. Part of the difficulty is the lack of a shared vocabulary to describe their culture or diagnose the elements of culture that may need to evolve. For many people, culture feels qualitative and ambiguous. Defining a culture is difficult because the manifestations are qualitative and the underlying drivers are usually hidden, built upon unconscious sets of shared assumptions that have developed over time. If you cannot see it, describe it, or measure it, of course it will be hard to manage it. As a result, it can be difficult to know if the culture is helping or hurting the business. Given this challenge, reinforcing the culture may seem particularly daunting to many organizations operating in a virtual environment.

In order to highlight how organizations can build and reinforce culture from a distance, it helps to use a model that can bring our recommendations to life. Based on many years of experience analyzing organizations, executives, and employees, our colleagues at Spencer Stuart developed a rigorous, comprehensive model to identify the key attributes of both group culture and individual leadership styles (see Figure 10.1). Eight characteristics emerge when we map cultures along two dimensions: *how people interact* (independence to interdependence) and their *response to change* (flexibility and stability). The spatial relationships also

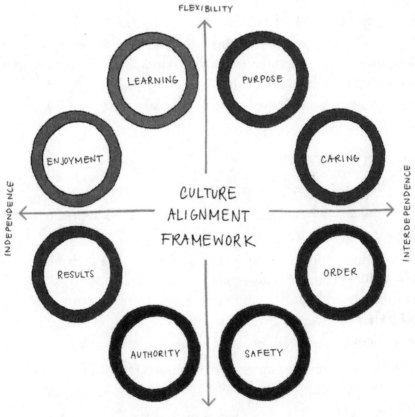

FIGURE 10.1
Source: Spencer Stuart

are important since proximate styles (such as safety and order or learning and enjoyment) will coexist more easily than those that are far apart.

The eight characteristics describe not only organizational culture – they also describe leaders' individual styles. For this reason, it's important that a leader's style and the organization's culture are in alignment; otherwise, conflict is likely. Each style represents a distinct and valid way to view the world, solve problems, and be successful in an organization. There are no inherently good or bad organizational cultures or individual cultural preferences; there are only good and bad fits, and cultures that can evolve to support aspirations and strategic objectives, or get in the way of them.

Our framework pinpoints eight primary and universal styles that shape all social and cultural behaviors. Any one company or individual has all eight of these styles but will emphasize some more than others. Some of the key characteristics of each style are as follows:

AUTHORITY

- Bold, decisive, dominant
- Focused on strength and influence; feels like a political arena
- People tend to be competitive and a high value is placed on dominance and power

RESULTS

- Achieving, driven, goal-oriented
- Focused on outcomes and winning; feels like a race or a competition
- People are driven to accomplish great things and a high value is placed on success and capability

ENJOYMENT

- Cheerful, unrestrained, instinctive
- Focused on fun and excitement; feels like a lively celebration
- People tend to do what makes them happy and a high value is placed on freedom and autonomy

LEARNING

- Open-minded, inventive, exploring
- Focused on exploration and creativity; feels like an adventure or journey
- People are willing to take creative risks and a high value is placed on discovery, growth, and openness

PURPOSE

- Idealistic, tolerant, balanced
- Focused on harmony and doing good; feels like a balanced ecosystem or a cause
- People are concerned for the long-term well-being of our world and a high value is placed on balance and having a greater perspective

CARING

- Warm, sincere, relational
- Focused on relationships and mutual trust; feels like a big family
- People tend to help and support one another, and a high value is placed on loyalty and collaboration

ORDER

- Reliable, cooperative, rule abiding
- Focused on stability and efficiency; feels like a smooth-running machine

- People tend to play by the rules and a high value is placed on order and respect

SAFETY
- Careful, prepared, realistic
- Focused on planning and caution; feels like a vault
- People tend to think ahead, and a high value is placed on predictability and caution

A purposeful, engaging culture is the foundation for any organization. Culture is linked to a variety of positive outcomes such as employee engagement and motivation as well as customer satisfaction.[2] However, one significant challenge confronting senior executives is how to build, maintain, and evolve their cultures virtually. How do you foster connectivity and leverage a virtual model to infuse your organization's sense of purpose and company culture? Mark Wetterau, chairman and CEO of Golden State Foods, said, "We are a culture-based organization and we instill this in the company. As a result, we need people here [in the office and at our facilities] to model and help them understand our culture, which can be difficult virtually." Larry Solomon, chief people officer at EPAM Systems, talks about infusing culture from afar. "How do we maintain culture and collaboration in the new environment? How do we keep an even playing field? I think out of sight, out of mind is not the case. We need to prove that this is not true." Hays Steilberg, CHRO of Bertelsmann, says their company has had an easier time shifting to remote work because so many employees are long-tenured. "We have substantial relationships, and trust has been established, which makes it easier," he said. Still, he worries if that's sustainable over long periods without face-to-face interaction. "As a species, humans are programmed to relate to each other on a physical and emotional basis," he said. "This is hard if we're not in an office."

Many organizations are grappling with how to shape culture in the world of virtual work. And CEOs and CHROs who feel most personally responsible for the cultural health of their companies express anxiety about the prolonged impact of remote work on their cultures. Owen Thomas is CEO of Boston Properties, the leading player in commercial real estate. He believes people became tired of work-from-home during the pandemic. "The collaboration and culture building that takes place in person began to unravel, as virtual connections turn out to be insufficient. With many companies, the bonds created through in-person mentorship, collaboration, and progress towards shared goals became harder to maintain in a remote environment."

But many are also adapting and succeeding at evolving their cultures to the virtual world. At HealthEquity, Natalie Atwood, vice president of People, said the shift has had a positive impact on their culture, as measured by net promoter scores in team member surveys. "Part of that goes back to everyone being level set since there is less of an 'us versus them' mentality," she said. "Our leaders have been transparent about decisions and people feel like they are informed, which they appreciate. We have been doing weekly virtual happy hours with all team members and after the first 30 minutes, we have a culture team, which has fun and games with prizes. Our executive leaders are all doing town halls so there is a feeling that we are all in it together. It's not 10 people in one location and one guy by himself in Arizona; everyone is on the same footing."

We want the emphasis of this chapter to be on practical insights as to how to evolve and maintain the best aspects of culture in a virtual world. Hopefully, you can start to leverage these tips to optimize your culture to a virtual or hybrid setting:

- Communication is essential to promote transparency, keep people informed, and reduce isolation. Welcome feedback and check in with people informally to ensure that you are accessible, which is important when working virtually. As Brian Dick, COO from Golden State Foods, shared with us, "We know less being remote since it is harder to know what people are going through. We must be more compassionate, patient, and understanding. We do not know what it is like to walk in their shoes on a particular day we are interacting with someone."

• John Donahoe, CEO of Nike, said in our conversation that virtual town halls have become a key tool to strengthen Nike's culture even as everyone worked remotely during the pandemic. "Every month I'm in front of 25,000 people live. We've been changing our core communications approach; when we do these Zooms we often have several thousand people on chat. So we now have the ability where anyone can ask a question and the communications flow is much more direct, transparent, and effective. It has been an enormous opportunity and given us a vehicle to drive culture change faster." Build culture into your virtual meetings. Use meetings to recognize people and share stories that reinforce your company culture. While it may be more difficult to do this virtually, it can be done effectively with focused effort. Boeing's David Calhoun added, "There is no doubt that there are advantages to having a face-to-face meeting to talk about values and dig into what a value means. You can't do this quite as well with videoconferencing and over a digital format. But I try to make up for this with increased frequency talking about our culture journey and making sure it's not overly programmed."

• Periodically take a pulse on how well you are communicating and reinforcing your organization's values through surveys and other measures and ensure people have resources to act. Ted Bloomberg, chief operating officer at HealthEquity, shared that he uses several proactive measures to infuse culture from a distance. "We recently developed a guide and assessment on virtual leadership as well as a virtual social connection website. We are also constantly looking for ways to engage the team with leadership directly. This year I hosted 24 livestreamed 'Happy Hours' that featured a variety of special guests and were typically attended by 500–1000 people. Finally, our dedicated culture team joins meetings to help ensure the time is spent in as engaging a way as possible."

- Hire with cultural intention. Consider how candidates map along the cultural dimensions of interdependence-independence and flexibility-stability. They don't have to fit neatly into the organization's current culture if you seek to evolve the culture. But hiring with keen awareness of an individual's style preferences can help you move the culture in the direction you seek. For example, one company we worked with set the goal of accelerating their pace of innovation. They realized that to enable this they had to move from a safety - and order-oriented culture (the lower right quadrant of the culture alignment framework shown in Figure 10.1) to a more learning-focused culture (the top left quadrant). So they put this into their hiring profile and assessed candidates along these dimensions, ultimately hiring a leader who was highest rated on learning and enjoyment to go along with results. Thinking strategically about hiring for culture also helps make progress on the diversity agenda. Diversity is about gender, race, and ethnicity, but it is also about diversity of thought and preferences. While it can be helpful to understand cultural fit, it is important to balance this in the broader context of diversity and inclusion.

- Culture, of course, starts with modeling from the top. Senior leaders need to be aware that their role modeling – how they live and what they do (more than what they say) – communicates the cultural norms and values of an organization more than any poster about mission and values. As a leader, practice what you preach, be as consistent as you can to leave no light between your words and actions, and find opportunities to share stories that reinforce the culture. If your organizational culture is high on purpose, for example, find ways to build on this theme. At HealthEquity, we learned through conversations that employees donate to a fund that helps colleagues who are in need (such as those who've experienced a fire or an illness). During just a few months in 2020, the company raised $100,000 to help colleagues.

- Prioritize meaningful work that gets people excited. Block calendar time for innovation workshops, lunch and learn sessions, inspirational external speakers (many of whom are more willing to speak over videoconference at team meetings), or feature customers to demonstrate the team's impact. At Cadence Design Systems, CEO Lip-Bu Tan said their culture is about creating trusted relationships with customers, and ironically, working virtually has made that easier. "We are spending more time with our customers, brainstorming and presenting to their teams. We've seen that customers are *more* open for meetings now," Lip-Bu said. "In the past, they were open to getting together, but it was always time consuming to set meetings. Now, everyone is one click away."

- Set up norms for how virtual teams will communicate and reexamine this over time as things shift. For example, what technology tools are best for the team? What is the etiquette for responding to one another when working remotely? Having explicit conversations about these topics not only builds culture and trust, but it also makes the team more effective.

- Create mentoring where "culture carriers" can coach others. One client uses "pair buddies" to give people time to build relationships. This company assigns them randomly and rotates them every six months.

- If your company culture is high on learning and growth, find ways to actively demonstrate this. For example, conduct virtual brainstorming sessions and find ways to ensure that people have opportunities to learn and develop.

- To reinforce your role modeling – and to remind you as a leader of those actions you need to continue to take – share your company's values and mission publicly. This also helps communicate your cultural values and helps people understand what is important in the organization. No company has gotten more mileage from talking publicly about its culture than Netflix. The Netflix culture deck[3] has been downloaded more than 20 *million* times. It's been used both as an offensive weapon (attracting talented people around the world who are inspired by their culture) and a defensive weapon (warning away people who are too far afield from its cultural norms).

- Communicate the importance of health and wellness. Some clients we work with have yoga sessions, mindfulness breaks and other activities to ensure work-life balance. Dominique Taylor from Axios mentioned codifying mental health days to encourage people to take them off. She also talked about having 5 p.m. events such as workouts to mark the end of the day since people were working long hours.

- Ensure that your leaders demonstrate empathy and compassion and that they regularly check in with people to show that they care. This is also essential to foster engagement and employee morale and retention. Lori Johnston, CHRO of Amgen, echoes the importance of empathy. "We changed our cadence working with our leadership team [after the pandemic set in] and moved quickly to check in with people. We infused empathy and the ability to be transparent right up front, and the impact was enormous. We did lots of small things right away to help people adapt and cope. We shortened meetings, shared meditation apps, and provided immense support. We knew that to create the environment to keep the culture ignited, we needed to respond quickly."

Party Time: Creative Ideas for Hosting Culture-Boosting Events

With so many organizations shifting to virtual teams, there is no shortage of advice on how to maximize engagement and productivity. However, the trend toward virtual does pose a vexing problem for a long-standing workplace tradition – the office party. Fortunately, there are creative ways to throw a memorable office party in a virtual context. Much like their in-person versions, these parties strengthen relationships and reward teams for a job well done.

One of our colleagues recently celebrated his retirement, so we had a virtual planning committee that took the lead on hosting a surprise party on video. We sent online invitations, and once we knew who was attending, we sent personalized swag bags to each attendee. The contents of the bag included our colleague's favorite foods, custom gifts with his name on it, as well as fun attire that people could wear for the party. The planning team compiled a video filled with messages from colleagues to wish him well. Then we had a virtual happy hour celebration where we played the video and gave some live speeches. It was a global event, and people were highly engaged.

We recognize that these virtual party tips may not work well in all virtual teams or company cultures. But we believe most organizations should give them a try, so we want to share some ideas that you can tailor to your company or team. Here are creative ideas for hosting the best virtual events.

Engage People in Planning

People are more likely to attend an event if they have a hand in its planning. A few rounds of simple online surveys can narrow down a list of potential activities to a more manageable number that everyone is excited about. Engaging people in planning helps avoid possible scheduling conflicts and allows the process to be culturally inclusive for more diverse teams.

Offer Prizes

It might sound like bribery, but there is nothing wrong with enticing team members to attend by offering virtual party favors or prizes like e-commerce gift cards. Setting up prizes for the winners of various party activities can ignite a little friendly competition and get the team excited.

Send Customized Online Invitations

Online invitations from sites like Evite or Punchbowl offer plenty of fun and creative ways to remind everyone about the virtual event. And since many of these invitations can be delivered for free, they're a quick and easy way to build excitement for the event.

Exchange Donation Gifts

Gift exchanges can be rather difficult in a virtual context (although delivering small gifts via Amazon and watching everyone open the box is a fun activity), so another approach is to let remote workers elect to make a donation to a charity of a co-worker's choice. There are plenty of ways to get creative with donation gifts. The Dale Carnegie Institute[4] once encouraged employees to think about what a co-worker was like as a child and then donate a toy that personified that person to a charity.

Kick Off with Team Video Content

A year in review video that covers the team's accomplishments can be a good way to get the event underway. Someone could also assemble a humorous blooper reel of memorable moments throughout the year or compile a series of song parodies recorded by each person.

Dress Up and Vote on the Best Outfit

Since virtual employees do not need to leave home to attend the event, they can go all out on creating a costume for the occasion. This could lead to some entertaining moments as everyone votes for the best outfit. At our colleague's retirement virtual party, people wore shirts with his face on them, fun boas, and other silly attire to get into the virtual spirit.

Submit Videos of Kids and Pets

Who doesn't love to see a toddler on Santa's lap or a dog wearing a little scarf? The team can share short videos to show what they are doing to celebrate the holidays with their family and friends (and pets!).

Share Memories and Traditions

Everyone has a funny holiday story. They may also have a unique tradition that sets their holiday experience apart from other families. Team members can take turns sharing both, which can not only provide plenty of laughs, but also help them get to know each other better.

Split into Groups for Games

While holiday games can be fun, virtual events suffer the same challenges as virtual meetings in that it's difficult for more than one person to talk at a time. Breaking into smaller groups to play games helps ensure that everyone stays engaged in the festivities and does not leave them looking to log off.

Give Out Awards

While a party may be a good time to reward people for good performance throughout the year, it is an even better opportunity to hand out fun awards. This would be a good time to recognize the person who loves singing along with the videoconference room's on-hold music or always knows how to perk everyone up.

Just because your team is virtual doesn't mean you cannot throw an event to remember. Many companies are already making virtual office parties an important part of their holiday traditions. With a little planning, the same tools that make virtual teams so effective can easily be deployed for a memorable virtual party.

The Bottom Line

- Modeling culture starts from the top. That's true whether leading in-person or virtually. Most leaders try to communicate more frequently when leading from a distance, and as the amount of communication increases, it's vital to make sure one's words and actions remain aligned.

- Leaders are concerned about how to ensure their corporate culture remains strong during all-remote work. Infusing culture into meetings, modeling behavior, hiring for cultural alignment, and using pulse surveys to measure how employees feel about the culture are all effective strategies.

- In-person office parties or informal gatherings play a key role in building culture, and it is challenging to transfer this to a virtual format. To improve the quality of your Zoom events, try engaging people in the planning, offering prizes, creating contests, and sharing memories or traditions. Some companies have dedicated culture teams to help plan virtual occasions.

Notes

1 "Culture Eats Strategy for Breakfast," Quote Investigator, https://quoteinvestigator.com/2017/05/23/culture-eats/.
2 Boris Groysberg et al., "The Leader's Guide to Corporate Culture," *Harvard Business Review*, January–February 2018, https://hbr.org/2018/01/the-leaders-guide-to-corporate-culture.
3 Lucas Shaw, "Netflix's Reed Hastings Conquered Hollywood With a PowerPoint Presentation", Bloomberg Quint, Updated September 8, 2020, www.bloombergquint.com/technology/what-s-in-reed-hastings-s-new-book-a-blueprint-for-how-he-conquered-hollywood.
4 Rick Lepsinger, "10 Creative Ideas for Hosting the Best Virtual Holiday Party," Best Practice in Human Resources, December 15, 2018, www.bestpracticeinhr.com/10-creative-ideas-for-hosting-the-best-virtual-holiday-party/.

Afterword: The Virtual Road Ahead

As this book went to press, in the winter of 2020–2021, the first doses of the COVID-19 vaccine were about to be administered. Offices had begun to reopen, albeit with fewer employees on premises, masks a regular part of one's outfit, and hand sanitizer dispensers everywhere. Business travel remained mostly dormant. It's a weird time, to say the least. We're writing these pages in what we *hope* are the final months of the crisis, so making predictions about the future of organizational life feels especially perilous.

Despite this uncertainty, we can say with conviction: The future will feature more virtual work, not less. Some companies will go to one of the extremes – either minimizing remote work to get as close to the way things were before the pandemic, or shedding all vestiges of in-office work with the attendant commuting, business travel, and relocations. But most organizations will find themselves somewhere in the middle in a hybrid model. In this future, a key driver of organizational success will be how effective leaders are in leading at a distance.

For David Solomon, Goldman Sachs CEO, the future is less about "going back to the way things were," and more about moving forward. "With our office interactions and all of the ways we will operate, the key message is that we'll have more flexibility

FIGURE A.1   Virtual road ahead.

in the way we'll work," he said. "It is much more powerful talking about this in a forward-looking way than trying to get 'back to normal.'"

At Starbucks, driven by a company-wide mindset of innovation and agility, they have completely reimagined the way they both work and operate in their workplace. While their folks were working from home, a year-long construction project was launched to create "a central gathering place where individuals interact, build relationships, propagate a culture of connection, and live the Partner Promise," with support for more flexible work options in the future.

Figuring out how fast and how far you are likely to go on this spectrum of virtual work will largely be a function of the sector in which you work, but other factors will play a role, too. Let's explore a few of them.

Some Sectors Are More Suited to Virtual Work

A McKinsey future-of-work study[1] confirms that remote work is likely to be more prevalent in industries such as technology, finance, insurance, and professional services. People whose work involves physically touching products will mostly continue to be on-site. As Carol Tomé, CEO of UPS acknowledged, most of her company's 500,000+ workers are front-line employees delivering packages or working in sorting facilities around the world. While there will continue to be tremendous innovation in how essential workers do their jobs, they will remain out on the world's roads or in the air delivering the packages – and in the process, helping many of us live and work from home. Many other companies also have essential functions that can't be done remotely.

"The hardest problems, and the most innovation, from the COVID-19 context have been in the field," said David Kenny, CEO of Nielsen. "Our courageous colleagues on the front line are used to being invited into homes to sign up panelists and install equipment. They kept things running through several innovations in how we operate – with recruiting, installing, and maintaining panelists all changing to more remote processes. Their fast and smart work kept the entire media industry operating with accurate measurements of their audiences."

Despite advances in automation and robotics, most of those jobs are not going to be remote anytime soon. Nor will many of the healthcare professionals, cable and telecom engineers, or many energy or factory workers.

The Gender Gap May Grow Even Wider

Despite the number of women who exited the workforce during the pandemic, we are hoping that the road ahead will bring

fewer exits and more reentry as things get back to some sem-
blance of normalcy. However, the most concerning aspect of this
shift will be the long-term impact on diversity and gender equity
at work. An article in *Time* magazine[2] talks about this disturbing
trend: 885,000 women left the workforce over a few periods of
several months in 2020, while only 216,000 men exited during
that same period. In addition, one in four women are cutting
back on hours or changing roles to ones that are less demanding.
The long-term consequences of this are unknown, of course, but
there is nothing good about them. Fewer women in the workforces increases gender pay gaps and the lack of diversity in senior executive roles.

Leaders Will Be More Selective with Business Travel

What will business travel look like in the new normal? While
answers to this question vary widely, it has become apparent
to many senior leaders that travel is not always necessary and
that they may be much more selective about when to travel in
the future. A McKinsey report[3] that examined the future of
business travel predicts that regional and domestic travel will
likely return first, and that in-person sales or client meetings
will take precedence over internal meetings. Projections by
several airlines estimate that approximately a quarter of pre-
pandemic business travel will be lost for the long-term, if not
for good. Southwest Airlines CEO Gary Kelly told CNBC
that the company will be focusing on leisure fliers because it
is likely to be 10 years before business travel returns to pre-
pandemic levels.[4]

Technology and Innovation Will Accelerate Virtual Work

When Darleen wrote her initial book in 2010, she interviewed executives from companies that were using Telepresence, which at that time was Cisco's innovative (and expensive) videoconferencing platform. Many leaders lamented that while Telepresence was great, it was not widely accessible, often reserved for senior executives. Since then, advancements in technology have continued to change how we work. Zoom, Teams, WebEx, and Blue-Jeans are now common household names, and these platforms have powered millions of remote workers and children engaged in distance learning. Online collaboration sites like Miro, Mural, and Notion have enhanced innovation and information sharing for remote employees.

As the shift to remote work continues to take hold, companies have had to improve their cybersecurity as employees are connecting remotely, often from their personal internet. People are also using numerous devices to communicate and share information, which makes remote work more flexible for employees but may lead to greater security concerns for organizations.

What will technology look like in the next decade? Technology companies will continue to focus on enhancing the user experience with videoconferencing. While these tools facilitate how we work, they also can be cognitively draining, as we discussed in Chapter 6 on virtual meetings. Will companies continue to build platforms that make it easier for people to drop into a virtual water cooler or café to have an informal discussion? Some technology companies are continuing to develop Virtual Reality software to mimic the office space environment. Organizations are experimenting with gamification to foster collaboration and fun, and to help deliver leadership development to a remote workforce. What role will artificial intelligence (AI) have in shaping technology? Overall, technology improvements will continue to shape the future of work and will make it easier to offset some of the drawbacks of not being together in-person.

While we believe that technology will continue to enhance how people communicate, interact, and collaborate virtually, we see technology as a prerequisite rather than a differentiator for effective virtual collaboration. Many high-performing virtual teams leverage technology in a strategic way, yet these teams would not be as effective without attending to the interpersonal, process, and structural elements that we know are essential for high-impact virtual teaming.

For Some People, Remote Work Will Be Unsustainable

Writing in the *Atlantic*[5] in October 2020, Amanda Mull contended that "Generation Work-From-Home May Never Recover." She argued that many people like the structure, routine, focus, and socialization provided by offices. She observed that some people value strict boundaries between their work and personal lives. Some people prefer to leave work at work; others have living situations (small residences, noisy roommates or partners) that make it extremely inconvenient to work remotely. The pandemic brought all of these issues to the fore – and as offices reopen, there are some people who will absolutely want to return. If they work at companies that decide to go all-remote, the odds are they will find someplace else to work.

In a Virtual World, Everyone Must Behave Like a Leader

Regardless of what resources an organization provides, the most constructive attitude that you as a leader and your employees might take going forward is described cleverly by Eric Barker, best-selling author and creator of the blog "Barking up the Wrong Tree: How to be Awesome at Life."[6] In a compelling post, "Congrats, you are no longer an employee. You are now the CEO of 'You, Inc.'" he shares his advice for helping all of us take control of our lives in these dynamic times:

1. **Be proactive, not reactive. Drive for and judge results, not hours.** "Now that working from home has given you more flexibility," Eric argues, "do the things that move the needle. Focus on the 20%."

2. **Know thyself and organize accordingly.** Given that we all have more freedom, many of the habits that used to unconsciously direct our behavior are gone. We need to replace them with new processes grounded in when, where, and how we do our best work.

3. **Create your new tailored CEO system.** "Systems beat goals," Eric says. "To succeed over the long haul, you want process goals, not outcome goals. Your process goals will be your daily activities, so put the tasks in your calendar and schedule everything accordingly."

4. **Manage your environment.** Do you have a setting at home where you're usually productive? "Go there," Eric advises. And similarly avoid the places where you are not productive. "Recreate the boundaries of the office in a new and improved way."

5. **Plan communication and feedback**. "If you don't already have regular check-ins planned with your boss," Eric comments, "do that, because you aren't going to randomly run into anyone at the water cooler anymore." And be prepared with a list of your accomplishments, questions, and requests for support. Also, it's essential to be planful about asking for feedback on how you're doing and where things stand.

The Hybrid Model Will Present New Kinds of Challenges

Our own research clearly confirms the increase in virtual work. Within the sectors that lend themselves to remote work, some organizations,[7] such as Facebook, Twitter, Zillow, and Shopify, are focusing on very flexible work-from-home options. But many other organizations will be implementing hybrid models. Verizon CHRO Christy Pambianchi illustrates the shift in the future state: "We won't return to the office the same way; we'll return to geographic hubs." Yet other companies, like Dropbox, are sensitive to the challenges that come with this hybrid model and have already put a stake in the ground by making its workforce *virtual first*. This means that its 3,000 employees will work remotely most of the time but sometimes go into an office, which they are calling "Dropbox Studios." Dropbox[8] opted to forgo a hybrid structure that would possibly create an uneven playing field among employees. The Dropbox Studios are for collaboration and gatherings, or collaborative spaces where people can engage with colleagues.

We already touched on the unique challenges that come with this hybrid model. As more companies embrace it, we expect new challenges will arise. Among them:

- There is a plethora of research on the importance of psychological safety at work, and we believe that creating this safety will become even more important as the hybrid approach grows. It may become harder to detect a loss of psychological safety in a virtual setting, and leaders need to be more deliberate about this when some employees are in the office and others are at home. Leaders need to focus on creating an equitable culture where people feel safe speaking up, voicing concerns, and feeling comfortable making mistakes.

- Cliques or subgroups form in physical offices, and they will become more evident in all-remote or hybrid cultures, too. To avoid the problems this can create, leaders must identify subgroups that may be forming, and take steps to avoid the erosion of trust they can create. In a hybrid model, when team members begin leaving remote team members out of discussions, collaboration and trust will suffer.

- One of the biggest concerns from employees about not being in the office is that "out of sight is out of mind." If organizations are promoting a hybrid model, it is critical to ensure that leaders treat people equitably. Do in-office employees get promoted more or receive more projects since they are "top of mind" to their boss. If leaders are serious about telecommuting and a hybrid model, they should role-model this by working from home part of the time.

- In a hybrid culture, where people aren't required to be in the office often, fears may arise that people who go in more frequently will enjoy career advantages. As Jane Datta from NASA articulated, "The risk is the hybrid environment where you lose the real benefits of being together and create a two-class system in the meeting where the people on screen aren't really participating as fully." To head off these concerns, HR leaders should track rates of promotion and career progression for employees working fully remote, fully in the office, and in the hybrid model. This will help ensure an even playing field and allay any fears.

- Some people will reduce their engagement if they're working remotely too often. In addition to tracking promotion rates, measure employee engagement over time to examine differences in the hybrid model. Our Spencer Stuart colleagues at Kincentric recommend periodic pulse surveys to monitor engagement and see what is working well and what can be improved.

Microsoft CHRO Kathleen Hogan raised a critical point about what many leaders have learned from the remote work experience. "Once we're in the promised land of being safe to come back to work," she said, "I think this all will be better in that we'll have navigated this incredible period, and we'll cherish being in person together. But we will have figured out that it doesn't have to be five days a week in the office, the way we used to."

* * *

Our journey together creating *Leading at a Distance* has been an exciting adventure. Even though we have been doing research and work in this area for more than a decade, the global pandemic thrust the issue of working remotely upon the world in one fell swoop. It's something with which all of us now have extensive personal experience. We hope that this book proves to be a useful tool as you successfully navigate the virtual environment in whatever form it unfolds for you and your organization.

Notes

1 Susan Lund et al., "What 800 executives envision for the postpandemic workforce," McKinsey Global Institute, September 23, 2020, www.mckinsey.com/featured-insights/future-of-work/what-800-executives-envision-for-the-postpandemic-workforce.

2 Abby Vesoulis, "'If We Had a Panic Button, We'd be Hitting it.' Women Are Exiting the Labor Force En Masse – And That's Bad For Everyone," *Time*, October 17, 2020, https://time.com/5900583/women-workforce-economy-covid/.

3 Andrew Curley et al., "For corporate travel, a long recovery ahead," McKinsey & Company, August 13, 2020, www.mckinsey.com/industries/travel-logistics-and-transport-infrastructure/our-insights/for-corporate-travel-a-long-recovery-ahead.

4 Kevin Stankiewidz, "Southwest Airlines CEO Gary Kelly told CNBC that the company will be focusing on leisure fliers because it is likely to be 10 years before business travel returns to pre-pandemic levels," CNBC, October 22, 2020, www.cnbc.com/2020/10/22/southwest-ceo-gary-kelly-on-return-of-business-travel-from-coronavirus.html.

5 Amanda Mull, "Generation Work-From-Home May Never Recover," *Atlantic*, October 2020, www.theatlantic.com/magazine/archive/2020/10/career-costs-working-from-home/615472/.

6 Eric Barker, "6 Things The Most Productive People Do Every Day," Barking Up The Wrong Tree (blog), accessed December 1, 2020, www.bakadesuyo.com/2020/11/productive-people/.

7 Jack Kelley, "Here Are The Companies Leading The Work-From-Home Revolution," *Forbes*, May 24, 2020,

www.forbes.com/sites/jackkelly/2020/05/24/the-work-from-home-revolution-is-quickly-gaining-momentum/?sh=7474533e1848.

8 Kathryn Vasel, "Dropbox is making its workforce 'virtual first.' Here's what that means," CNN Business, updated October 13, 2020, www.cnn.com/2020/10/13/success/dropbox-virtual-first-future-of-work/index.html.

Acknowledgments

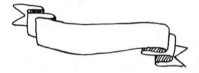

Acknowledgments from Jim Citrin

Leading at a Distance, my eighth book, underscores what I have long shared with anyone who has an interest in how a book comes to be. It is no solitary literary endeavor in isolation in the woods; it is a collaborative community effort. As I wrote in the Preface, this book never would have been conceived without the expertise and passion of my co-author, Darleen, but more importantly her commitment and dedication to this project. While managing a demanding client service portfolio (we're partnering on a major global financial services CEO succession engagement, so I see it first-hand) and being a hands-on mom to energetic kids during a WFH year, she somehow managed to find all the hours on weekends, early mornings, and late nights to translate all of her research and experience into words on hundreds of pages, bringing an intensity and responsiveness that was inspiring.

Equally importantly, two of my closest Spencer Stuart colleagues and friends, Hannah Ford and Ashley Zaslav, leaders in our CEO Practice, agreed to dive into the project with their characteristic enthusiasm from day one. Experts in CEO succession and engagement management, Hannah and Ashley really should be given their due as full co-authors of *Leading at a Distance*. They participated actively in scores of CEO and CHRO interviews, led external research on all the topics, wrote up stories that we shared in their must-read internal Spencer Stuart weekly newsletter, "CEO Debrief," and helped me write many editions of my LinkedIn newsletter, "Leading at a Distance." They helped design and execute our Virtual Leadership surveys, along with our also brilliant, analytical, and creative colleague Will Dowling. Hannah and Ashley also managed all the moving parts in this effort, kept us on track, and drove the project management to hit all our ambitious deadlines. Second most importantly, they helped write and edit the manuscript, weaving in their expertise and personal experiences, working remotely from Bermuda (Hannah) and Washington, D.C. (Ashley), with the incredible support and partnership of their amazing husbands, Mike Ford and Jordan Zaslav, and the beauty of Jala and Zoe ever present in their homes. Most importantly, Hannah and Ashley, along with the other core members of our small CEO Practice Dream Team, Melissa Stone and Maddi Conlin, are the epitome of what we wrote in this book about highly effective virtual teams. We all tried to learn from and apply the insights from this book into our intense day-to-day lives working at a distance. I believe over the course of this past year our team has operated at a higher level and with more fun and effectiveness that ever before. The principles and tactics in this book really work! Part of this Dream Team, but meriting a special callout for appreciation, is my assistant, Karen Steinegger, who for the last 27 years has been my business partner. We've been through thick and thin in our professional work at Spencer

Stuart and in the twists and turns of life, and all of my clients and candidates, as well as friends and family, know Karen as the brains of the operation.

I love what we do at Spencer Stuart, and it's all made possible by our clients. As interesting and clever as we may be, without our clients and all of the incredibly exciting mandates for CEO and board searches and CEO successions and leadership advisory projects with which we are trusted, the world's most compelling and high-level leaders would not find it particularly interesting spending time with us. Our flywheel (to quote my business and management book inspiration Jim Collins) is quite simple: We have the best clients in the world trusting us with the most important leadership mandates; that in turn helps us have access to and add value on a highly trusted basis to the world's most important and inspirational business leaders. With those relationships, developed in some cases over nearly three decades, we are able to win the best and most important client engagements. To illustrate, the vast majority of interviews, anecdotes, and insights woven throughout *Leading at a Distance* came from dialogues with and access to our treasured clients. Thank you all for your partnership and trust.

I am also appreciative of Dan Roth and his talented editorial and content team at LinkedIn, which has given me a platform to test and share ideas and get feedback from members of its global community. I am proud to be a LinkedIn Influencer and am humbled by the one million followers that have chosen to take their precious time reading my posts and offering thousands of thoughtful comments and insights.

Thanks to the wide and consistent support from our Spencer Stuart colleagues far and wide, who have supported this project: our managing partner, Ben Williams; our chairman, David Daniel; our North American Leader, Kim McKesson; and our Commitments Committee. We were able to share previews of the book with key internal audiences and thanks to our friends and partners Greg Sedlock and Rick Routhier, leader of our Global Technology, Media, and Telecom Practice, and our incredible Stamford office, respectively. We benefit every day from our wonderful marketing and content team, led by Ben Machtiger and with the hands-on excellence of Tim McNary, Emily Ford, Whitney Calkins, and Beth Hoffman, who have all been enormously helpful in turning this book from concept to reality. Similarly, we are deeply appreciative of the creative genius of Keith Scott, our colleague in our Leadership Advisory Services Practice, who brought his design thinking expertise to bear throughout the book and in my LinkedIn "Leading at a Distance" newsletter.

We would also like to thank the incredibly talented team at John Wiley, led by Zach Schisgal. Zach has believed in this project from the very start, and we have benefitted from the hugely value-added work of Dawn Kilgore, who has been a dedicated partner throughout the process. We also appreciate the profound support and commitment of the entire organization and for that we want to thank Brian Napack, CEO of John Wiley & Sons. One of the most important contributions to the shaping and coming together of this book has been Dan McGinn, executive editor at *Harvard Business Review*. Dan is one of the top editors and reporters in the world of business. In addition to overseeing the magazine's feature well and team of editors who produce its long-form articles (several of which I have co-authored), he was a thought partner and editor to "Leading at a Distance" on special assignment in the fall of 2020. He added incredible value and sharpness to everything we did. Thank you, Dan. While we knew Dan, the inspiration for recruiting him to our team came from our friend and partner Rafe Sagalyn. Anyone in the world of nonfiction and business books knows Rafe, the world's number one literary agent. I've worked with Rafe since 1997, when he took a shot on an unknown executive recruiter with an ambitious idea to identify and profile the world's top CEOs. That became my first book, *Lessons from the Top*, co-authored with the single most distinguished Spencer Stuart leader ever, Tom Neff (who is still crushing it in the market for CEOs and boards!). Rafe and his incredible partner and protégé, Tia Ikemoto from ICM, have been our sounding boards and partners throughout this entire journey.

I'd like to thank my amazing kids, Teddy and his fiancé, Natalia; Oliver and his incredible girlfriend, Erin; and Lily and her magnificent partner, Sara, who have been sources of joy and inspiration forever, and never more than during the lockdowns of 2020. Finally, I'd like to thank my life partner, Lindsay, to whom this book is dedicated, for her constant love and support.

Acknowledgments from Darleen DeRosa

I am exceptionally grateful for Jim's partnership. Jim has been an incredible advocate, mentor, friend, and a tremendous source of inspiration. Despite an insanely busy schedule, Jim's passion, creativity, and commitment were evident during every single step of this journey. Not surprisingly, as an expert on world-class leadership, Jim helped us build the most talented virtual team. Jim, it has truly been a pleasure to collaborate with you on this exciting project. I cannot thank you enough for your advice and ongoing support, for which I am eternally grateful.

Hannah Ford and Ashley Zaslav have been incredible partners on our virtual book team. In essence, this book would not have been possible without their energy and commitment to this project. We are lucky to have such smart and talented colleagues who are willing to contribute their time. I am extremely grateful for their partnership in every aspect of this book, from writing, research, graphics, creative content, and chapter ideas, to amazing virtual project management. Every successful virtual team needs brilliant and passionate colleagues like Ashley and Hannah to truly thrive.

Will Dowling was a fantastic partner on all of our surveys, research, and analytics. Will and our amazing colleagues at Kincentric led all of the research and analysis, drawing tremendous insights from the data. Kimberley Lawrence voluntarily joined our project team to artfully curate the content editing, as well as to lead client permissions.

I am grateful to our talented partners at John Wiley & Sons, Zach Schisgal and Dawn Kilgore, who have been fantastic thought partners. Dan McGinn, executive editor at *Harvard Business Review*, joined our virtual team in the last month of the book process to coach and guide us on issues ranging from chapter titles and key content decisions to other best practices. With little time to spare, Dan jumped on board and provided tremendous insights to shape the book. When Jim and I presented the book concept to Jim's literary agent, Rafe Sagalyn, he was immediately on board and offered great ideas and advice throughout the entire journey. Thank you to our former Spencer Stuart colleague Monica Watt for her creativity, skillful drawing, and contagious enthusiasm on this project.

I would like to thank Rick Lepsinger, my former business partner and co-author of our first book on virtual teams. Rick was supportive when I first raised the idea for the original book, as well as the concept of designing leadership development programs on topics related to leading from a distance, more than a decade ago. Rick and I brought these ideas to life through leadership development solutions that we offered to hundreds of clients during our partnership at OnPoint Consulting, where Rick and I collaborated for more than a decade on best practices for virtual leadership.

Meghan Powell has been a member of our high-performing virtual team for more than a decade. She has become an expert on this topic, playing an instrumental role in our research projects and client engagements. I am beyond grateful for Meghan's ongoing partnership.

I am also extremely grateful for my talented assistant, Aimee Hurtado, who managed to brilliantly juggle countless numbers of book interviews and client work.

I would like to personally thank Patrick Hynes, our global Leadership Advisory Services practice leader, and Nicolas Albizzatti, who leads Leadership Advisory for North and South America, for their ongoing support and collaboration. There are countless colleagues at Spencer Stuart to thank, including Brett Clark-Bolt, David Elbaz, Stacey Peck, Janine Ames, Kathy Schnure, Noah Shamosh, and Rick Routhier. When we presented the idea to Ben Machtinger, our talented strategy and marketing leader, Ben was immediately on board with the idea and shaped all marketing efforts. I am personally grateful to Ellen Kumata and Colleen Gentry, our wonderful partners at Cambria Consulting, who helped us with book interviews and client introductions.

Finally, I am exceptionally grateful to my husband, Joe, for his unwavering support, and my children, Natalie and Drew. I always end up writing a book over the summer, which means missing a number of events and working most nights and weekends. They provided constant encouragement along this adventure. I am also very appreciative of the endless support from my dad, who always told me that I can accomplish anything. To my tribe – you know who you are – thank you for your support and encouragement.

About the Authors

Jim Citrin leads Spencer Stuart's CEO Practice and serves on the firm's worldwide board of directors. A distinguished expert on leadership, CEO succession, and career success, Jim has published eight books including the worldwide best-sellers *You're in Charge, Now What?*, *The Five Patterns of Extraordinary Careers*, and *The Career Playbook*.

Throughout his twenty-seven years at Spencer Stuart, Jim has completed 800 CEO, board director, and top management searches for the world's leading media, technology, consumer, retail, financial services, healthcare, and diversified companies, as well as some of the most important global not-for-profit and educational institutions.

Jim graduated Phi Beta Kappa from Vassar College and served as a trustee on their board for twelve years. He also served as a trustee and is now a trustee emeritus at Wesleyan University (from where two of his children graduated). Currently, Jim is on the boards of the International Tennis Hall of Fame, the Johnny Mac Tennis Project, and Girl Effect. He obtained his MBA from Harvard Business School, graduating with distinction. Jim started his career as an analyst at Morgan Stanley and after business school was an associate at Goldman Sachs and then spent five years as a management consultant at McKinsey in the U.S. and France before joining Spencer Stuart in 1994.

Jim lives in Connecticut and has three children, Teddy, Oliver, and Lily.

Also by James M. Citrin

Lessons from the Top (with Thomas J. Neff)

Zoom

The Five Patterns of Extraordinary Careers (with Richard A. Smith)

You're in Charge – Now What? (with Thomas J. Neff)

The Dynamic Path

You Need a Leader – Now What? (with Julie Hembrock Daum)

The Career Playbook

Darleen DeRosa, Ph.D., is a consultant in Spencer Stuart's Stamford office and a member of the Healthcare and Leadership Advisory Services practices. Darleen brings more than 15 years of consulting experience, with deep expertise in talent management, executive assessment, virtual teams, and leadership development. Darleen works with leading companies to facilitate selection, succession management, and leadership development initiatives. She is a trusted advisor to CEOs, CHROs, and boards.

Prior to joining Spencer Stuart, Darleen led OnPoint Consulting for more than 12 years. Earlier, she was an executive director in the assessment practice at another leading international search firm, where she conducted assessments of senior executives across industries. Before that, Darleen served as assessment practice leader for Right Management Consultants, responsible for the practice's growth in the Northeast region. In addition, Darleen was a clinical researcher at the Yale School of Medicine. She began her career at AT&T in human resources.

Darleen earned her B.A. in psychology from the College of the Holy Cross and her M.A. and Ph.D. in social/organizational psychology from Temple University. Darleen is the co-author of *Virtual Success: A Practical Guide for Working and Leading from a Distance* (with Richard Lepsinger), as well as other book chapters and journal articles on leadership.

Index